Strong Roots, Flourishing Futures

Strong Roots, Flourishing Futures

Matthew Edward Petchinsky

Strong Roots, Flourishing Futures: The Risks of Over-Coddling in Child Development

By Matthew Petchinsky

Introduction: The Gentle Trap

In the warmest corners of a caregiver's heart lies the instinct to protect. It is a beautiful, deeply human drive—to wrap children in love, to guard them from pain, and to ensure their path is smooth, happy, and safe. But what happens when that protective instinct becomes overextended? What happens when the shelter becomes a cage, and comfort becomes a crutch?

We are living in a time where parenting and caregiving have undergone a radical transformation. Today's world is saturated with fear—fear of failure, fear of danger, fear of inadequacy. In response, many well-meaning adults have turned parenting into a 24/7 mission to ensure their children never struggle. This has given rise to a growing phenomenon: **over-coddling**.

Over-coddling is not the same as loving or nurturing a child. Instead, it is the **excessive shielding from discomfort, difficulty, decision-making, and failure**. It shows up as doing everything for the child—solving their conflicts, making their choices, excusing all mistakes, or constantly stepping in to prevent them from experiencing any form of pain, disappointment, or frustration. What begins as care often slides quietly into overcontrol, and that overcontrol stunts more than just independence—it stunts growth.

Here lies the great paradox: the very love that seeks to strengthen a child can end up weakening them. When we rob children of the chance to struggle, we also rob them of the opportunity to build grit, emotional stamina, and problem-solving skills. The result is a generation of children—especially teens and young adults—who appear confident on the surface but collapse under pressure, retreat from responsibility, or remain stuck in a state of arrested development. They may fear trying anything new unless success is guaranteed. They may rely heavily on parents for guidance well into their twenties. They may crumble at the first sign of failure, unprepared for the unpredictable nature of adult life.

This book is about **that gentle trap**—how it happens, why it happens, and how to break free from it.

Throughout the following chapters, we'll explore the **short- and long-term consequences** of over-coddling, from early childhood through adolescence and into adulthood. We will dive into the psychological, emotional, social, and even neurological effects that emerge when children are deprived of challenges and autonomy. You will read about real-life scenarios, developmental research, and recognizable patterns seen in over-coddled individuals.

More importantly, this book will offer **healthier alternatives**. It will not shame parents, grandparents, teachers, or guardians. Instead, it will guide them back to a balanced form of care—one that honors protection without sacrificing preparation. You will learn how to raise children with **strong roots**, capable of weathering storms, navigating difficulty, and growing into confident, competent adults.

Because the goal of parenting is not to walk ahead of a child and remove all obstacles. The goal is to **walk beside them, equip them, and then watch them walk on their own—stronger for having learned how.**

Chapter 1: What Is Over-Coddling?

The first step toward preventing over-coddling is recognizing what it is—and what it isn't. Many caregivers conflate love with control, safety with avoidance, or nurturing with rescuing. But **over-coddling is a distinct and measurable pattern** that, over time, undermines the very development it hopes to support.

Defining Over-Coddling: The Illusion of Care Without Growth

Over-coddling refers to the act of excessively protecting a child from challenges, discomfort, conflict, or failure in a way that **inhibits their emotional, social, and cognitive development**. This can include constantly intervening in their decisions, shielding them from natural consequences, doing tasks they are capable of doing themselves, or suppressing their emotional responses before they've had a chance to process them.

It is often driven by **fear, guilt, or an idealized image of perfect parenting**—not malice. The caregiver may believe they are providing safety, love, or help, but in reality, they are unintentionally sending a message to the child:

"You are not capable. You need me to survive. The world is too scary or hard for you."

This message, repeated subtly over time, **erodes confidence** and trains a child to depend on the adult's input for every decision, reaction, or task. It prevents the natural building blocks of independence from forming.

Over-Coddling Across Different Parenting Styles

Over-coddling doesn't look the same in every household. It can show up across **many different parenting styles**, often dressed in the language of "helping," "guiding," or "protecting."

1. Authoritarian Over-Coddling

- May seem paradoxical, but some strict parents over-coddle by **controlling every decision**—from the child's schedule to their friendships.
- Children may be "protected" from failure because parents don't allow them to take risks or explore beyond rigid boundaries.
- These children often **lack confidence** in thinking independently.

2. Permissive Over-Coddling

- Caregivers may say "yes" to everything to **avoid tantrums, tears, or emotional discomfort**.
- Children are protected from all emotional upset, but **never learn limits** or how to manage disappointment.
- This creates emotionally fragile children who **expect the world to cater to them**.

3. Helicopter Parenting

- This style involves **constant hovering**, solving all problems before they arise, and **intervening immediately** at the first sign of difficulty.
- The child may appear successful or well-organized but often **relies entirely on the parent's presence** to function.
- This can lead to burnout for the parent and **learned helplessness** in the child.

4. Snowplow (Lawnmower) Parenting

- Caregivers **eliminate all obstacles** in advance: difficult teachers, challenging projects, or tough social situations.
- The child never experiences consequences, problem-solving, or **earned confidence**.
- As adults, these children may **panic when life isn't curated for their comfort.**

Each of these patterns has different tones, but the same core outcome: **a child who is deprived of opportunities to struggle, grow, and trust themselves.**

Healthy Nurturing vs. Over-Coddling: A Critical Distinction

Let's be clear—**nurturing is essential**. Children need emotional warmth, safety, love, and encouragement. But nurturing should empower, not restrict.

Healthy Nurturing	Over-Coddling
Encourages trying new things	Discourages risk for fear of failure
Allows space for mistakes	Prevents mistakes by doing everything for the child
Offers emotional support *during* difficulty	Removes all difficulty to avoid emotional distress
Respects the child's ability to problem-solve	Assumes the child is incapable or too sensitive
Builds resilience	Breeds dependency
Prepares the child for reality	Shields the child from reality

Healthy nurturing **validates emotions but still encourages growth**. Over-coddling invalidates growth by assuming the child's emotions mean they're not ready or capable.

Early Warning Signs in Toddler and Preschool Years

The seeds of over-coddling are often planted early—sometimes as soon as a child begins walking, talking, or asserting preferences. While some behaviors may seem harmless or even humorous in toddlers, they can grow into chronic dependency patterns if not addressed.

Look for these early signs:

◈ **Task Interference**

- Parents frequently **intervene during play** to "fix" how a toy is used or to prevent frustration.
- The child resists doing tasks like dressing themselves, cleaning up, or feeding themselves—even when developmentally capable.

◈ **Avoidance of Emotional Discomfort**

- Caregivers **distract from or shut down tears** instead of helping the child process feelings.
- Tantrums are met with immediate compliance to avoid further distress, rather than boundaries.

◈ **Lack of Choice Opportunities**

- Parents **make every decision** (what to eat, wear, do) without involving the child.
- The child never experiences the natural consequences of their own choices.

◈ Excessive Soothing or Avoidance of Frustration

- Caregivers rush in at the first sign of difficulty (e.g., puzzle pieces not fitting, minor falls).
- The child is rarely encouraged to **try again or find another way**.

◈ Over-Apologizing or Over-Explaining

- The parent excessively **justifies boundaries or decisions**, fearing the child's emotional response.
- This teaches the child that **emotions are too powerful or dangerous** to handle.

Why It Matters Early

Toddlerhood and preschool years are when key traits such as autonomy, problem-solving, resilience, and emotional regulation begin to take root. When over-coddling starts early, it **hijacks this development** and replaces it with fragile coping strategies.

A two-year-old who cannot tolerate frustration may become a ten-year-old who quits easily.

A preschooler who's always told what to do may become a teenager unable to think independently.

An over-soothed child may grow into an adult who needs external validation to feel okay.

Chapter 2: Helicopters and Snowplows – Modern Parenting Pitfalls

The journey from nurturing to over-coddling is often paved with love, concern, and cultural pressure. Today's parents live in a world that bombards them with messages about danger, competition, and the need to optimize every moment of their child's life. Caught in a storm of anxiety and expectation, many parents unknowingly adopt extreme control mechanisms that not only smother their child's independence—but also **prepare them for nothing but dependency**.

Two of the most recognizable patterns that have emerged in the last few decades are **helicopter parenting** and **snowplow parenting**. These are not simply cute metaphors—they are indicators of how modern parenting has evolved into a cycle of over-involvement, anxiety, and emotional micromanagement that severely inhibits a child's autonomy.

◈ Helicopter Parents: Hovering at Every Turn

Coined in the early 2000s, the term **"helicopter parent"** refers to caregivers who hover constantly over their child—ready to swoop in at the first sign of trouble, disappointment, or failure.

Key traits include:

- Monitoring every interaction, assignment, or challenge with extreme vigilance.
- Frequently **intervening in schoolwork**, disputes with peers, or even choices about clothing, food, or hobbies.
- Micromanaging routines and "rescuing" from emotional distress rather than coaching through it.

While helicopter parenting may stem from love, it sends a harmful message:

"I don't trust you to handle life. I have to do it for you."

Over time, this erodes self-trust. Children under helicopter parenting grow up second-guessing their choices, fearing mistakes, and **needing constant validation** before acting.

◈ Snowplow Parents: Clearing All Obstacles Before They Exist

An evolution of the helicopter parent, the **snowplow parent** goes a step further—not only hovering, but actively removing all potential roadblocks before their child ever faces them.

Signs of snowplow parenting:

- Intervening to **change a teacher** if the class is too hard or the child is uncomfortable.
- Calling employers to help teens get jobs or promotions.
- Constantly advocating to alter consequences (grades, punishments, setbacks).

The intent is to protect a child's path, but the result is devastating: children raised this way never **build internal coping mechanisms**. They **expect the world to rearrange itself** for them.

By never letting the child experience discomfort, frustration, or healthy failure, snowplow parents create young adults with extremely low distress tolerance—many of whom **collapse at the first taste of real-world expectations**.

◈ The Cultural and Social Media Storm Fueling the Epidemic

Modern parenting is not happening in a vacuum. Several **social, cultural, and technological forces** have made it much harder to resist the urge to over-coddle:

◈ Fear-Based Media and "Parental Shame Culture"

- The 24/7 news cycle floods parents with stories of abduction, bullying, cyber danger, and social failure.
- The constant exposure to worst-case scenarios creates a **heightened sense of risk**, even when the odds are statistically low.
- Parenting decisions are judged harshly—publicly. A single online post or schoolyard conversation can result in **criticism or shaming**, causing many to overcompensate.

◈ Social Media Comparison Traps

- Instagram, TikTok, and Facebook have created a dangerous illusion: perfect parenting, perfect children, perfect lives.
- Parents are inundated with curated images of overachievement, luxury childhoods, or "gentle parenting gurus."
- This leads to **performance-based parenting**, where parents try to avoid any blemish in their child's life or emotions—**not for the child's well-being, but to avoid perceived failure**.

◈ Academic and Economic Pressure

- College admissions have become an arms race. From kindergarten, children are funneled into elite programs, test prep, and curated experiences.
- Snowplow parents believe that any misstep could cost their child their future—so they **remove every perceived threat** to the child's resume or reputation.
- Children are taught to **chase perfection**, not progress.

◈ How These Patterns Evolve in School-Age Years

Once a child enters school, the helicopter and snowplow behaviors often **intensify**. Parents begin managing entire school experiences as if they were project managers.

Common evolutions:

- **Over-helping with homework**, often doing assignments for the child.
- Attending parent-teacher conferences with a goal of **negotiating or defending**, not listening or supporting.
- Scheduling every moment of a child's day to prevent boredom, challenge, or free time.
- Immediately stepping in during any social difficulty—never letting the child **resolve their own friendships or conflicts.**

This deprives the child of learning essential life skills: navigating challenges, coping with rejection, managing time, solving interpersonal issues, and recovering from setbacks.

By the time the child is a teen, they have **rarely practiced these skills independently**, which leads to a sudden identity and competence crisis. They may appear smart or well-behaved but feel **utterly unprepared to face the world alone.**

◈ Impact on Autonomy and Problem-Solving Skills

At its core, over-coddling disrupts one of the most vital stages of human development: the creation of a **strong, separate self**. Autonomy isn't about rebellion—it's about the **ability to function confidently in the world**.

When a child is constantly rescued or directed:

- They fail to develop **initiative**.
- They fear making mistakes, so they **avoid decisions** entirely.
- They feel incapable when faced with a problem that hasn't already been pre-solved for them.

The ability to solve problems requires **practice, exposure to complexity, and safe failures**. When that's stolen from them, children grow up with what researchers call **"learned helplessness"**—the belief that they can't influence outcomes, so they don't try.

◈ A Kind Intention with a Costly Outcome

The most dangerous thing about over-coddling is that it **doesn't look dangerous**. It looks like help. It feels like love. And in the short term, it brings calm, comfort, and relief—to both child and parent.

But this short-term peace breeds long-term weakness.

As cultural, technological, and emotional pressures increase, more and more parents fall into this **gentle trap**—a form of parenting that **prepares the child for nothing but more parenting**.

Unless we step back, reflect, and realign our priorities, we are raising a generation that will struggle deeply in relationships, careers, and personal growth. Not because they aren't smart or loved—but because they were never given a chance to **stand alone and become capable**.

Chapter 3: The Brain That Doesn't Struggle, Doesn't Grow

We often associate love with comfort, but in the world of human development, **comfort can be the enemy of growth**. While it's natural to want to spare children from pain and failure, shielding them from all struggle **blocks the brain's ability to build strength, adaptability, and resilience**. Put simply: the brain that doesn't struggle, doesn't grow.

In this chapter, we explore **the science behind challenge, stress, and failure**, and how the developing brain depends on these very experiences to build long-term success. Discomfort isn't just something children can handle—it's something their **neurological system was designed to encounter and grow from**.

◇ **Cognitive, Emotional, and Executive Functioning Require Struggle**

Human development is not just about absorbing information; it's about processing reality, navigating problems, regulating emotions, and making independent decisions. These functions—especially **executive functioning**—are built **through tension, challenge, and adaptation**.

What Is Executive Functioning?

Executive functioning includes:

- Working memory
- Cognitive flexibility
- Impulse control
- Emotional regulation
- Planning and problem-solving

These abilities begin forming in early childhood but continue developing **well into the mid-20s**, particularly in the **prefrontal cortex**, the part of the brain responsible for higher-order thinking and self-regulation.

However, this region of the brain **cannot grow in a vacuum**. It develops **in response to challenge**. When a child solves a puzzle, calms themselves after frustration, resolves a conflict, or figures out how to recover from failure, their brain is literally **rewiring and strengthening**.

Without exposure to these experiences, neural connections that support independence, regulation, and resilience **remain underdeveloped**.

◈ The Neuroscience of Stress Tolerance and Resilience

Contrary to popular belief, **not all stress is harmful**. In fact, scientists distinguish between three types of stress:

1. **Positive Stress**
   - Short-term, manageable stress that promotes learning and growth.
   - Examples: Starting a new class, performing in a recital, or losing a game.
2. **Tolerable Stress**
   - More intense stress that can be buffered with support.
   - Examples: Moving homes, a difficult exam, or a school conflict.
3. **Toxic Stress**
   - Prolonged, unbuffered stress that overwhelms a child's coping system.
   - Examples: Abuse, neglect, or chronic trauma without support.

What over-coddling often does is **eliminate the positive and tolerable stress**, treating them as if they were toxic. But without exposure to these safe stressors, the child **never builds the neurological tolerance** required to handle life's inevitable challenges.

Neuroscientific research shows that **cortisol and adrenaline**, hormones released during stress, help the brain **encode learning, increase attention**, and even **promote memory consolidation**—but only when experienced in healthy doses and followed by recovery.

So, when parents rush to fix, prevent, or remove all difficulty, they're not just making life easier—they are **interfering with biological systems designed to strengthen the brain**.

◈ The Consequences of Avoiding "Necessary Discomfort"

A child who never experiences distress **never learns how to soothe themselves.**

A teen who's never allowed to fail **never learns how to try again.**

An adult who's never had to solve their own problems **will always wait for someone else to fix them.**

These are the long-term effects of over-coddling through a neuro-science lens:

1. Delayed Emotional Regulation

- When parents constantly calm, distract, or remove discomfort, children don't learn how to **name, manage, or process their own emotions.**
- This leads to teens and adults who panic under pressure or seek instant relief (often through unhealthy habits).

2. Underdeveloped Problem-Solving Pathways

- The brain strengthens connections that are used repeatedly.
- If a child never navigates difficulty, the **neural circuits for persistence and adaptation remain weak**.

3. Low Distress Tolerance

- Without early and consistent exposure to safe stress, children become hypersensitive to everyday challenges.
- This results in **meltdowns, avoidance, anxiety, or emotional shutdowns** even when facing minor setbacks.

4. Poor Frustration Tolerance and Quitting Behavior

- Children who are protected from struggle tend to **give up quickly**, avoid anything hard, and often **lack the motivation to improve**.
- They equate discomfort with failure, rather than progress.

5. Chronic External Validation Seeking

- Over-coddled children often rely on parents to determine if their actions are "right."
- As adults, they become dependent on others for approval, direction, and even emotional stability.

◈ Why Discomfort Is Biologically Necessary for a Flourishing Future

Biologically, humans evolved in **environments that required daily adaptation**. Children learned through doing—through trial and error, challenge and consequence, cooperation and conflict.

Our bodies and brains are not wired for endless comfort. In fact:

- **Bones grow stronger under pressure.**
- **Muscles grow through resistance.**
- **Brains grow through problem-solving and recovery.**

Neuroplasticity—the brain's ability to rewire and strengthen over time—**thrives on meaningful challenge**. Without those inputs, the brain becomes **rigid, anxious, and reactive**, rather than flexible, confident, and resilient.

By avoiding discomfort, we are doing something far more dangerous than we realize:

We are preventing our children from becoming who they are capable of being.

◈ Moving Forward with Growth in Mind

The goal is not to traumatize children or abandon them to struggle alone. The goal is to offer **"supported challenge"**—experiences that stretch them while still providing a secure emotional base.

Ask:

- Can my child do this on their own with time or effort?
- Am I rescuing them to calm myself or truly because they're overwhelmed?
- How can I offer encouragement **without interference**?

When we embrace the discomfort of watching our children struggle, we allow their **brain and body to do the work of growing**. The reward is not just survival—it's capability, creativity, and confidence.

Chapter 4: Fragile Self-Esteem and False Confidence

In a world where every child gets a trophy, where effort is optional and praise is plentiful, we find ourselves facing a paradox: **a generation of children raised to always feel good—now struggling the most when they finally face the real world.**

Parents and caregivers often shower children with praise, believing it will boost their confidence and protect their self-worth. But what happens when praise is **given without effort, challenge, or authenticity**? What happens when a child is celebrated simply for existing, and not for persevering?

The answer is one of the hidden costs of over-coddling: **fragile self-esteem and false confidence**.

These are not simply emotional traits—they are **developmental outcomes**, shaped by the environment and messaging a child receives from birth through adolescence. And when praise is offered as a substitute for growth, the long-term result is not empowerment—it's emotional dependency, fear of failure, and an inability to measure one's own worth without external applause.

◈ Praise Without Effort: The Entitlement Trap

One of the most common mistakes made by over-coddling caregivers is the **overuse of praise**—especially when that praise is disconnected from genuine effort, persistence, or accomplishment.

Examples of misguided praise:

- "You're so smart!" (even when no thinking was required)
- "You're the best player!" (after a weak performance)
- "You did amazing!" (when the child didn't even try)

This kind of praise creates a distorted feedback loop:

1. The child receives praise regardless of effort.
2. The brain **associates praise with identity**, not action.
3. The child begins to expect recognition for minimal input.

Over time, this reinforces **entitlement**, where children come to believe they deserve praise, rewards, or special treatment **simply for existing**—not for showing up, growing, or pushing through difficulty.

In the real world, this belief **collides hard with reality**. Teachers, coaches, bosses, and peers don't reward mediocrity. And when over-praised children don't receive instant approval, their confidence **cracks like glass**.

◈ Fragile Self-Esteem: When Confidence Depends on Comfort

Healthy self-esteem is built through:

- **Experiencing challenge**
- **Taking risks**
- **Failing and trying again**
- **Receiving accurate feedback**

Fragile self-esteem, by contrast, is built on:

- **Empty praise**
- **Shielding from failure**
- **Over-involvement**
- **Constant reassurance**

Children with fragile self-esteem may seem confident, but they often:

- **Avoid difficult tasks** because they fear not looking "smart" or "talented."
- **Become easily discouraged** at the first sign of struggle.
- **Crave perfection**, but give up when perfection isn't guaranteed.
- **Overreact to criticism**, interpreting it as a personal attack.

This fragility is not due to low ability—it's due to **low resilience**. Because their self-worth has always been externally confirmed, they never learned to **build inner validation** or tolerate temporary setbacks.

◈ The Rise of Validation Addiction

In today's digital culture, the craving for external validation is not only reinforced—it's **magnified and monetized**.

Over-coddled children are especially susceptible to what psychologists now call **"validation addiction"**—a psychological dependence on praise, approval, likes, or affirmation to feel okay.

The symptoms include:

- Constantly asking, "Did I do it right?"
- Needing someone to observe or praise every small task.
- Obsessing over social media approval or comparisons.
- Emotional crashes when not praised or noticed.

This pattern starts early. When children are raised in environments where their **worth is always reflected back to them** through adult validation, they never learn how to **self-assess or self-soothe**. Their self-image becomes a fragile mirror held by others.

In adolescence, this often shows up as:

- Excessive people-pleasing.
- Obsession with appearance or popularity.
- Avoiding new opportunities unless praise is guaranteed.
- Deep anxiety over not being "good enough."

And in adulthood, it can lead to:

- **Impostor syndrome**
- **Workplace burnout**
- **Over-dependence in relationships**
- **Fear of rejection or criticism**

◈ Why Children Become Afraid of Trying and Failing

Over-coddled children often learn one dangerous idea early on:

"If I fail, I am not lovable."

When praise is conditional—when it only comes after success, or when success is faked through exaggerated affirmation—failure begins to feel **emotionally unsafe**.

Children who are never allowed to fail:

- Avoid hard tasks to **protect their ego**.
- Develop **performance anxiety**, fearing public mistakes.
- **Downplay effort** ("I didn't even try") to save face if they don't succeed.
- Use perfectionism as a mask to avoid vulnerability.

Ironically, the very praise meant to build self-esteem ends up creating **a fear of authentic growth**, because growth always involves messiness, setbacks, and perseverance. But if a child has only experienced comfort, they interpret discomfort as danger rather than development.

◈ False Confidence vs. True Self-Worth

It's easy to mistake loud, outgoing, or charming children as confident. But real confidence isn't about volume—it's about **resilience**.

False Confidence	True Self-Worth
Based on praise	Based on effort
Crumbles with failure	Grows from failure
Seeks approval	Seeks mastery
Avoids risk	Embraces growth
Looks perfect	Embraces progress

False confidence is a costume. It gets tested—and often torn—when the real world offers feedback, rejection, or failure. And many children raised in over-coddled environments **aren't emotionally prepared for that test**.

◈ The Hidden Cost of Praise Without Perseverance

The greatest danger of over-coddling is that it **gives children the illusion of competence without the substance of capability**. When self-esteem is inflated without being earned, and confidence is built without discomfort, we raise children who **look prepared but feel lost**.

They are not weak or broken—but they are untested.

They are not unlovable—but they are **uncertain how to love themselves when they fall short**.

As caregivers, it's not our job to remove failure from their lives. It's our job to **frame failure as feedback**, to praise effort over ease, and to teach them that their worth is not defined by perfection—but by perseverance.

Chapter 5: The Social Consequences – Awkward, Anxious, and Isolated

The early years of a child's life are not just about learning to walk, talk, or write. One of the most vital developmental tasks is **learning how to be with other people**—to communicate, compromise, express needs, resolve disagreements, and collaborate toward shared goals. These social skills are not instinctive; they must be practiced, often through conflict, messiness, and emotional discomfort.

But when children are over-coddled—when parents speak, decide, and even feel on their behalf—this learning process is stunted. The result? A child who is academically capable but **socially delayed**. A teen who is outwardly confident yet **emotionally fragile in relationships**. An adult who may succeed in solitude but **struggles deeply with connection, criticism, or conflict**.

In this chapter, we'll explore **the social consequences of over-coddling**, focusing on what happens to children who haven't developed **emotional independence**—and why many of them grow up to feel **awkward, anxious, or isolated in a world that expects self-regulation and social agility.**

◈ The Missing Practice: When Parents Speak and Act for the Child

It starts early. A toddler reaches for a toy, but the parent hands it to them before they can ask. A preschooler argues with another child, but the parent intervenes and mediates. An elementary school child forgets homework, but the parent emails the teacher. A teenager receives a grade they don't like, and the parent arranges a meeting to argue on their behalf.

Each time this happens, a message is encoded:

"You are not capable of navigating your world. Let me do it for you."

Over time, this approach prevents the development of core **social muscles**:

◈ What's Lost:

- **Conversational confidence**: Kids don't learn how to speak up for themselves or ask questions.
- **Self-advocacy**: They don't know how to request help or clarify confusion with teachers or peers.
- **Conflict resolution**: They avoid disagreements or rely on adults to solve every dispute.
- **Boundaries and consent**: They struggle to say "no" or recognize when their own needs aren't being respected.

⬧ **The Struggle with Peer Conflict and Compromise**

All healthy relationships require some form of tension: disagreement, negotiation, discomfort, compromise. These moments are **not problems—they are practice** for emotional maturity.

But over-coddled children rarely get that practice.

Instead of navigating playground arguments, classroom team projects, or friend drama themselves, they are either:

- **Removed from the situation entirely** ("We'll find you a new friend/class/teacher"), or
- **Directed exactly how to respond**, with scripts and solutions fed to them by adults.

The result? Children who:

- Crumble under peer conflict.
- Blame others quickly and take little responsibility.
- Expect others to always yield to them, since they're used to being rescued or prioritized.
- Feel intense anxiety about confrontation and **avoid it at all costs**.

And yet, confrontation, negotiation, and disagreement are all **normal and necessary** aspects of social life. Without skills to navigate these, over-coddled children **withdraw or dominate**—both of which create distance in relationships.

◈♀ **What Happens When Emotional Independence Never Develops**

Emotional independence means being able to manage your own feelings, handle distress, and engage with others without constantly outsourcing your emotional needs. This is built through age-appropriate emotional challenges, mistakes, and self-regulation.

When over-coddling prevents children from experiencing discomfort, they never build these tools. Instead, they:

- Expect others to **mirror and manage their emotions.**
- Struggle to tolerate others' emotions, especially strong or negative ones.
- Misinterpret neutral or ambiguous interactions as **personal rejection.**
- Feel overwhelmed in social settings where **feedback or disagreement is present.**

As they grow into teens or young adults, they often:

- Have difficulty making and keeping friends.
- Feel deeply misunderstood or left out—even when they're included.
- Experience **performance anxiety** in group settings.
- Retreat into isolation, gaming, or curated online environments where social risk is minimal.

Their isolation is not always visible—it's internal. Many feel **alone even in a room full of people** because they lack the confidence, tools, or resilience to connect meaningfully.

❖ School and Beyond: A World That Expects You to Stand Alone

Modern school environments, especially in the later grades, begin expecting students to:

- Self-advocate to teachers.
- Collaborate on group projects.
- Manage homework and schedules independently.
- Handle social challenges and disagreements without constant adult mediation.

But over-coddled children often find these expectations **jarring and overwhelming**. What seemed like a "perfect" childhood—full of love, praise, and smooth sailing—becomes a liability when the real world doesn't bend to their needs.

By high school, these students may:

- Refuse group work or participation.
- Rely on parents to email teachers or tutors.
- Avoid social situations entirely.
- Experience increased anxiety, depression, and even **school refusal** behaviors.

In college or the workplace, the gaps grow wider. Without emotional independence and social fluency, even highly intelligent individuals may:

- Drop out of college after minor setbacks.
- Avoid applying for jobs that involve people.
- Be seen as "difficult," "entitled," or "emotionally immature."
- Experience loneliness that isn't just circumstantial—but developmental.

◈ Awkward, Anxious, and Isolated: The Hidden Cost

Social success isn't about popularity. It's about feeling safe being yourself while also understanding others. It's about connection, communication, and **tolerating the tension that comes with being human**.

Over-coddled children often miss this entirely. Their early relationships are overly managed. Their disappointments are minimized or redirected. Their emotional experiences are filtered, narrated, and sanitized.

So when they are finally required to stand on their own—**in classrooms, relationships, jobs, or public life**—they freeze. Not because they're broken. But because they were never prepared.

They become:

- **Awkward**, because they haven't practiced spontaneous interaction.
- **Anxious**, because they fear making a mistake.
- **Isolated**, because they find the emotional labor of connection too daunting.

◈ Rebuilding Social Roots: What Children Really Need

Children don't need perfect social experiences. They need **authentic ones**:

- Disagreements that they are allowed to resolve.
- Friendships that ebb and flow, without adult interference.
- Rehearsal in the real world, with real people, in real time.

They need room to feel uncomfortable—without being rescued.
They need boundaries—without being controlled.
They need guidance—without being overridden.
They need to know that emotional pain is **not the end of connection**, but part of the growth process.

Chapter 6: Anxiety and the Avoidance of Adulthood

Adulthood is often painted as a rite of passage into freedom—independence, decision-making, self-expression, and the thrill of carving one's own path. But for a growing number of young people today, **adulthood isn't an exciting milestone—it's a looming threat**.

They stall. They withdraw. They stay in childhood bedrooms, skip college, avoid jobs, delay relationships, and shut down when the world asks them to grow up. This is not laziness. This is **crippling anxiety and an aversion to independence**, deeply rooted in **over-coddling during their formative years**.

In this chapter, we'll examine how children who are shielded from struggle and decision-making **become teens and young adults who feel emotionally paralyzed by the very concept of adult life**. You'll see how over-coddling is directly tied to rising rates of anxiety, depression, and what psychologists now refer to as **"failure to launch."** Supported by real-world studies, we'll uncover what's really behind this generational crisis—and how we can reverse it.

◈ From Over-Coddled to Overwhelmed: How Avoidance Takes Root

When children are repeatedly protected from struggle, discomfort, and decision-making, they don't learn how to self-regulate, problem-solve, or manage responsibility. Instead, they learn to fear it.

These children become **used to someone else solving problems**, making plans, and softening reality for them. They become highly sensitive to emotional discomfort, overreliant on external validation, and chronically unprepared to tolerate stress.

By the time they enter adolescence—a period that demands increasing independence—they begin to **panic, shut down, or avoid altogether**.

They are not broken. They are **unpracticed**.

Common signs of growing avoidance:

- Extreme difficulty making decisions (even small ones)
- Panic attacks over academic or social challenges
- Refusal to get a part-time job or driver's license
- Avoidance of social situations or new environments
- Extended dependency on parents for tasks they could do themselves
- Refusing to apply to colleges or take career steps

⬦ The Link Between Over-Coddling and Mental Health Issues

Over-coddled children are more likely to develop:

- **Anxiety disorders**
- **Depression**
- **Perfectionism**
- **Low self-efficacy** (belief that they can't influence outcomes)
- **Avoidant behavior patterns**

Numerous psychological studies confirm this connection.

⬦ Study #1: The Parental Overprotection Index (University of Queensland)

A longitudinal study of over 2,500 young people found that **children exposed to overprotective parenting** had:

- Higher anxiety levels in adolescence
- Greater dependency in relationships
- Poor coping skills under stress

⬦ Study #2: Journal of Adolescence – "The Cost of Catching"

This study coined the term **"catching" parenting**—when caregivers preemptively "catch" a child before they can fall. Findings showed:

- Children of "catchers" reported **more depressive symptoms** as teens.
- They developed **lower frustration tolerance** and **reduced intrinsic motivation.**
- As adults, they were more likely to **avoid challenges** in both work and relationships.

◈ **Study #3: American Psychological Association – "Helicopter Parenting and Emerging Adult Anxiety"**

This study followed college freshmen and found that students with helicopter parents:

- Struggled significantly more with time management, emotional regulation, and confidence.
- Were **twice as likely** to experience symptoms of clinical anxiety and panic disorders.

◈ The Teenage Crisis: Fear of Growing Up

Adolescence is meant to be a time of experimentation, boundary-testing, risk-taking, and identity formation. It's the developmental bridge between childhood and adulthood. But for over-coddled teens, it becomes a **crisis point**.

These teens:

- Avoid jobs, dating, or driving.
- Panic over independent responsibilities like managing money or applying to college.
- Delay important milestones (getting licenses, seeking independence, exploring passions).
- **Withdraw into safe, controlled environments**—often virtual (video games, online communities, curated social media bubbles).

Rather than seeing adulthood as empowering, they associate it with:

- **Pressure they don't feel equipped to handle**
- **Judgment they haven't learned to process**
- **Uncertainty they were never allowed to face**

Adulthood becomes something to be feared, not embraced.

◈ Failure to Launch: When Development Freezes

The term **"failure to launch"** is used to describe young adults who are developmentally stuck—unable to transition into independent living, employment, or relationships.

But this term oversimplifies what is often a deep-rooted developmental wound. These individuals aren't lazy—they are **crippled by a lifetime of disempowerment**. They were praised without challenge, protected from decisions, and buffered from the emotional discomfort that builds real-life competence.

What failure to launch often looks like:

- Living at home indefinitely with no plan to leave
- Avoiding employment or academic steps
- Spending excessive time in fantasy-based or digital worlds
- Relying on parents or caregivers for basic decision-making
- Deep insecurity masked by withdrawal or apathy

◈ The Brain on Avoidance: A Vicious Loop

When a child is protected from stress, their brain doesn't learn to manage it. As a result:

1. The prefrontal cortex (decision-making and self-regulation) remains underdeveloped.
2. The amygdala (fear and threat detection) becomes **hypersensitive**.
3. Stressful situations trigger **panic or freeze responses**, reinforcing avoidance.

Each time avoidance "works" to relieve anxiety, it strengthens the habit:

- "I didn't apply for the job → I didn't panic → That means avoidance works."
- "I didn't attend the group project → I didn't feel humiliated → I should keep avoiding."

This loop creates what's known in psychology as a **"safe bubble"**—but over time, the bubble shrinks until even basic adult tasks feel overwhelming.

◈ **Shielding from Distress = Aversion to Independence**

Emotional maturity doesn't come from knowing how to avoid pain—it comes from knowing how to **move through it**.

When over-coddling prevents discomfort:

- Children don't learn how to tolerate stress.
- Teens don't develop problem-solving or emotional flexibility.
- Young adults **fear responsibility**, because it's unfamiliar and terrifying.

They don't avoid adulthood because they're lazy—they avoid it because they've been taught it's **unsafe**.

◈ Restoring Readiness: What Helps

Fortunately, this pattern can be interrupted. Even young adults who seem lost can **rebuild their capacity for independence and resilience** with the right approach:

1. **Gradual Exposure to Responsibility**
   - Start small: budget a weekly meal, make their own appointments, handle one recurring chore.
   - Celebrate effort, not outcome.
2. **Normalize Discomfort**
   - Teach that anxiety, stress, and even failure are not emergencies—they are **growth markers**.
   - Share personal stories of setbacks and resilience.
3. **Encourage Emotional Ownership**
   - Replace rescuing with coaching. Help them name, feel, and move through emotions.
   - Ask, "What's your plan?" instead of giving them one.
4. **Limit Enabling Behaviors**
   - Stop solving problems they can solve themselves.
   - Resist the urge to be their emotional shield or spokesperson.
5. **Therapeutic Support**
   - Cognitive Behavioral Therapy (CBT), exposure therapy, and resilience coaching have all been shown to help young people rewire fear-based avoidance.

◈ Letting Go to Let Them Grow

Over-coddling begins with love—but unless we **step back**, that love turns into a form of **unintentional imprisonment**. We cannot protect our children into adulthood. We can only **prepare them**.

True support isn't about catching them every time they fall. It's about teaching them **how to get back up on their own.**

Chapter 7: The Loss of Problem-Solving Muscles

Problem-solving is one of the most essential life skills a person can possess. It's what allows us to navigate the unexpected, adapt to change, make informed decisions, and take responsibility for outcomes. But problem-solving—like any skill—requires **practice, challenge, and repetition** to develop. When children are over-coddled, they are protected not just from harm but from **opportunity**—the opportunity to struggle, think, act, fail, adjust, and grow.

This chapter explores how over-coddling **systematically weakens the problem-solving "muscles"** that children need to thrive, and how that loss creates a dependency cycle that carries into adulthood. When children are raised to believe someone else will fix, decide, or shield them from difficulty, they enter the adult world **lost, unprepared, and emotionally unequipped** to meet its demands.

◈ The Death of Daily Decisions

Every child is born with a natural curiosity and a desire to try, explore, and figure things out. But in many over-coddled households, **even the smallest decisions are outsourced to adults**:

- What to wear
- What to eat
- What to play
- What to say
- When to do it
- How to feel about it

The result is not structure—it's **learned passivity**. A child who has never been allowed to make small, low-risk decisions cannot possibly gain the confidence or skill to make larger ones later.

◈ When children don't decide:

- They **lack agency**: They feel powerless in their own lives.
- They **fear choices**: Because choices come with consequences, and consequences are unfamiliar.
- They **become dependent on authority**: Waiting for someone else to tell them what's right, what's next, or what's allowed.

And when life inevitably demands independent decisions—especially in high school, college, or adulthood—they freeze.

◈ Removing Obstacles = Removing Growth

Children don't grow by having everything go right. They grow by:

- Figuring out how to fix something that broke.
- Learning what doesn't work.
- Discovering how to recover from a mistake.
- Feeling the satisfaction of solving a challenge independently.

But over-coddled children rarely face obstacles on their own. Instead:

- Parents step in at the first sign of struggle ("Let me do it for you.").
- Problems are solved before the child even notices them ("I already called the teacher for you.").
- Mistakes are prevented rather than processed ("Don't worry, I'll take care of it.").

This **short-circuits the developmental process**. Without repeated exposure to problem-solving situations—no matter how small—the brain **fails to build the neural architecture needed for persistence, critical thinking, and innovation**.

It's not just about solving puzzles or tying shoes. It's about developing the **belief** that "I can figure this out." That belief, repeated and reinforced over time, becomes the foundation of resilience and competence.

◈ The Psychology of Learned Helplessness

Psychologist Martin Seligman's work on **learned helplessness** revealed a troubling truth: when individuals are consistently denied the opportunity to act independently or feel that their actions have no impact, they begin to **give up—even when solutions exist.**

Over-coddled children are **primed for this condition**. They learn early that:

- Trying is optional, because someone else will finish the job.
- Struggling is bad, because it means they're failing.
- Success must come quickly—or it isn't worth the effort.

This creates a **mental model of helplessness** that becomes deeply ingrained. By the time they reach adolescence or early adulthood, many have internalized this belief:

"If I don't already know how to do it, I probably can't."

◈ The Dependency Cycle: How It Begins and Why It Persists

Over-coddling creates a self-reinforcing loop:

1. **The parent prevents struggle.**
   The child doesn't make decisions or solve problems.
2. **The child doesn't build skills.**
   Their confidence and resilience never form.
3. **The child becomes anxious or avoidant.**
   They fear doing things independently or wrong.
4. **The parent sees the anxiety and steps in again.**
   More problems are solved *for* the child instead of *with* the child.
5. **The cycle repeats.**

Each repetition of this loop deepens the child's dependence and **weakens their problem-solving ability**. This is not merely behavioral—it becomes **neurological and emotional conditioning**.

Eventually, the child expects others to manage the mechanics of life:

"What should I do?"

"Can you fix it for me?"

"Tell me what's right."

"I don't know how—I never have."

◈ A World That Demands Initiative

In school, the shift begins around age 10: teachers expect students to take more responsibility. By high school, independent study, time management, and social navigation become critical. In college and the workplace, initiative is not optional—it is **assumed**.

But over-coddled teens and young adults:

- Often **fail to initiate tasks** unless someone instructs them.
- Wait for perfect conditions, **avoiding mistakes at all costs**.
- Abandon efforts early, unsure how to push through confusion.
- Constantly ask for help—even for tasks within their ability.
- Experience **panic** when no adult authority is present to "check their work."

This lack of experience with natural problem-solving tasks leaves them **emotionally brittle and functionally dependent**.

In the real world, they don't just feel anxious—they feel **lost.**

◈ Rebuilding Problem-Solving Muscles

The good news: the brain is plastic, and **problem-solving ability can be rebuilt**—at any age.

But the process requires discomfort, patience, and a shift in mindset from both the child and the parent. It begins with **small, low-stakes decisions** and builds from there.

◈ Practical Tools:

- Ask questions instead of giving answers:

"What do you think you should do?"
"How could you try that a different way?"

- Encourage reflection after struggles:

"What worked? What didn't? What will you do next time?"

- Let natural consequences occur safely:

"If they forget their lunch, they'll feel hungry—but they'll remember next time."

- Praise persistence, not speed:

"I'm proud of how long you kept trying."

- Resist the urge to "fix it faster":
  Growth requires time. Let them fumble.

◇ **The Real Victory Isn't the Solution—It's the Belief**

What we want our children to walk away with isn't just answers—it's a deep, unshakable belief:

"I can handle hard things."
"I don't have to know everything to start."
"I can figure it out."

This belief is the real goal of parenting—not perfection, not protection—but preparation. Children who grow up solving problems become adults who can **lead, adapt, persist, and thrive**.

Chapter 8: Struggling in the Workforce

For decades, society has operated on a core assumption: once children reach adulthood, they'll be ready to function in adult environments—managing jobs, taking initiative, meeting deadlines, solving problems, and navigating authority. But today's employers, educators, and mentors are seeing a troubling trend: **many young adults entering the workforce are not ready for these expectations.**

They may have strong academic records. They may be intelligent, well-spoken, and even charming in interviews. But beneath the surface lies a fragile infrastructure—one built on **over-coddling, emotional avoidance, and underdeveloped problem-solving muscles.** The result? A growing population of young adults who **crash hard** when faced with the pressures of real-world employment.

This chapter explores what happens when over-coddled children grow into **functionally dependent employees**—and why so many of them struggle, burn out, or quit when the workplace demands initiative, feedback, or emotional resilience.

◈ Weak Problem-Solving Muscles in a High-Demand World

In the previous chapter, we discussed how over-coddled children never build their internal problem-solving "muscles." These young people are rarely exposed to challenges that require:

- Independent decision-making
- Trial-and-error experimentation
- Long-term planning
- Emotional regulation in the face of frustration

As children, they were protected. As teens, they were managed. But in the workforce, there's no one standing beside them to:

- Solve problems before they occur
- Rescue them from consequences
- Soften critical feedback
- Organize their workday
- Interpret emotions for them

So when challenges arise—as they inevitably do in any job—they **freeze**, **panic**, or **withdraw**.

◈ Common Patterns of Workforce Struggle

The following are recurring behavioral patterns seen among over-coddled young adults in professional environments:

◈ Lack of Initiative

- Waiting to be told exactly what to do
- Fear of making decisions without supervisor approval
- Reluctance to act without a safety net
- Paralysis in the face of ambiguity or open-ended tasks

◈ Inability to Handle Feedback

- Taking constructive criticism as a personal attack
- Emotional shutdown or defensiveness
- Avoiding performance reviews, meetings, or direct communication
- Seeking constant reassurance rather than improvement

◈ Poor Time and Task Management

- Struggling to prioritize tasks
- Missing deadlines due to procrastination or anxiety
- Overestimating abilities and underdelivering
- Becoming overwhelmed by routine responsibilities

◈ Discomfort with Authority and Accountability

- Viewing authority figures as oppressive rather than instructional
- Expecting praise for showing up, not for producing results
- Blaming others for mistakes or unmet expectations
- Crumbling when held to standards of professionalism

◈ Low Frustration Tolerance

- Quick burnout when tasks become repetitive or stressful
- Avoiding challenges rather than facing them
- Emotional overreaction to minor problems or course corrections
- Quitting jobs impulsively when things feel "too hard"

◈ From Over-Coddled to Underprepared

What causes these patterns? A lifetime of unintentional over-protection. Let's break down how coddling in childhood sets the stage for workplace failure:

Coddling in Childhood	Consequence in the Workplace
Decisions made for the child	Fear of acting independently
Mistakes prevented or erased	Inability to recover from failure
Praise without effort	Entitlement to rewards for minimal work
Tasks completed by adults	Lack of task management skills
Emotional distress avoided	Panic under pressure
Authority softened or overridden	Resistance to feedback or structure

This transition is often jarring. Many young adults report feeling **confused, unsupported, and overwhelmed**, despite holding jobs that are considered "entry level" or "low pressure." The issue isn't the job—it's their **lack of internal coping structures**.

◈ **Employers' Growing Concerns: What the Data Shows**

Across industries, managers and business leaders are expressing growing concern about a gap in what many refer to as **"soft skills"** or **"professional maturity."**

Surveys and Observations:

- A 2019 survey by the Society for Human Resource Management (SHRM) found that **over 51% of employers** said young workers lacked critical thinking and problem-solving skills.
- A LinkedIn Workplace Learning report in 2021 ranked **emotional intelligence, communication, and adaptability** as top missing skills in the emerging workforce.
- Employers consistently cite issues like:
  - **Low resilience under stress**
  - **Inability to adapt to change**
  - **Poor follow-through**
  - **Lack of grit**

These aren't technical gaps—they're **developmental ones**. Grit, creativity, and resilience are **forged in childhood through friction**, not delivered via textbooks or training seminars.

◈ Why Many Young Adults Crash at Work

Let's look at what happens psychologically when over-coddled young adults step into a workplace:

1. Cognitive Overload

They've never had to **juggle multiple responsibilities** without support. Even simple multitasking becomes overwhelming, leading to exhaustion and poor performance.

2. Emotional Dysregulation

Feedback, missed deadlines, or interpersonal friction trigger disproportionate emotional responses. Some experience **panic attacks**, others withdraw entirely.

3. Identity Collapse

Work is often the first time these young adults are held accountable. Without praise, hand-holding, or permission, they feel stripped of identity:

"Who am I if I'm not being told I'm doing well?"

4. Avoidance Behaviors

Rather than confronting their skill gaps, they:

- Avoid assignments
- Call out sick frequently
- Ghost employers
- Quit impulsively

The workplace becomes an arena of shame rather than growth.

◈ What They Needed—and Still Can Build

This isn't the end of the story. Young adults raised in over-coddled environments can **still build resilience, initiative, and problem-solving skills**—but it takes honest feedback, delayed gratification, and structured discomfort.

◈ What Helps:

- **Real consequences**, not softened outcomes
- **Supportive but firm mentorship**, not emotional catering
- **Skill-building workshops**, especially in communication, time management, and emotional regulation
- **Opportunities to fail safely**, reflect, and try again
- **Gradual independence**, replacing "rescue parenting" with coaching and accountability

Parents who wish to course-correct can still help—not by fixing—but by **encouraging perseverance and modeling how to navigate struggle with grace and grit.**

◈ Final Thoughts: Competence Over Comfort

The workforce doesn't reward comfort. It rewards **adaptability, creativity, follow-through, and the ability to handle pressure**—all skills that begin in childhood but must be reinforced through practice, not protection.

Over-coddled young adults don't lack potential.

They lack **practice**.

They lack **preparedness**.

They lack the lived experience of **doing hard things without being saved**.

And that's something we can still change.

Chapter 9: Relationship Struggles and Emotional Fragility

When Protection Turns Into Dependency in Love and Connection

By the time over-coddled children reach young adulthood, the effects of their upbringing are no longer confined to school or work—they begin to **weave into their personal and romantic lives**, often with heartbreaking results. Relationships require vulnerability, compromise, boundary-setting, and emotional endurance. But if a young adult has been shielded from struggle, coached through every emotion, and insulated from natural conflict, they arrive in relationships **without the tools to withstand emotional turbulence.**

This chapter explores how emotional and functional fragility—cultivated by over-coddling—**spills over into friendships, dating, and long-term partnerships**. These individuals often expect others to mirror the caregiving roles of their parents: to stabilize their mood, resolve their conflicts, and act as emotional regulators. When this doesn't happen, they spiral—into blame, panic, isolation, or collapse.

◈ **Emotional Dependence Masquerading as Intimacy**

Over-coddled teens and young adults often **confuse emotional neediness with emotional intimacy**. Because they were taught (either explicitly or subtly) that:

- Their feelings needed to be "managed" by others,
- Discomfort must be removed quickly,
- And others are responsible for their emotional stability,

...they enter relationships with **deep emotional dependency**.
In romantic partnerships, this often manifests as:

- **Expecting constant reassurance** ("Do you still love me?" "Are you mad?")
- **Melting down during minor disagreements**
- **Needing immediate conflict resolution**, even when space is healthy
- **Taking everything personally**, even when it's not about them

These behaviors do not stem from selfishness. They stem from a **lack of emotional training**. The over-coddled young adult was never taught to:

- Sit with discomfort
- Self-soothe
- Navigate differences
- Manage distress without external intervention

Instead of a partnership between equals, their relationships often become **caretaker-and-dependent dynamics**, which can suffocate the connection and lead to cycles of dysfunction.

◈ Expecting Others to "Fix" Their Feelings or Solve Their Problems

One of the most damaging effects of over-coddling is the belief that **other people are responsible for your emotional state**. As children, these individuals were not encouraged to identify and regulate their own feelings—they were often distracted from them or rescued emotionally by caregivers.

This creates adults who:

- Expect their partner to **"make them feel better" instantly**
- Rely on others to **define their mood**
- Blame others for **their own discomfort**
- Feel abandoned if their partner asks for space or emotional boundaries

Rather than learning how to manage emotional waves **with their partner**, they **place the responsibility for their entire emotional world on the other person**—an unrealistic and unfair burden.

◈ The Breakdown of Boundaries

Healthy relationships require **boundaries**—a mutual respect of space, identity, and emotional separation. But for many over-coddled young adults, boundaries are **experienced as rejection or abandonment**, because they were never modeled or practiced in childhood.

As children:

- Boundaries were often blurred (parents did everything, made all decisions)
- Emotional enmeshment was normalized (if I'm upset, everyone must fix it)
- Autonomy was rarely encouraged

So as adults, they may:

- **Invade emotional space** ("Why didn't you text back right away?")
- **Fear independence** in the relationship ("Do you really want to be alone right now?")
- **Collapse when separated**, even briefly
- **Interpret personal space or self-care as rejection**

The inability to handle healthy separation leads to **clinginess, control, and emotional volatility**, all of which strain the relationship and eventually push the partner away.

◈ Breakups and Conflict: Emotional Fragility Exposed

When emotionally dependent individuals experience breakups, relational tension, or arguments, their reactions are often **extreme**. Without emotional resilience, every disagreement feels like disaster. Every hurt feels permanent. Every breakup feels like the end of the world.

They may respond with:

- **Panic attacks or breakdowns**
- **Desperate attempts to fix things instantly**
- **Aggressive blame or guilt-tripping**
- **Complete emotional shutdown or isolation**

This response isn't immaturity—it's **emotional inexperience**.

They were never allowed to struggle emotionally in childhood, so they never learned that:

- Emotions are temporary.
- Pain does not mean permanent damage.
- Conflict can be productive.
- Disagreements do not equal abandonment.

Without these core beliefs, every emotional wave **feels like drowning**—and the partner becomes either the lifeguard or the enemy.

◈ When Partners Become Parental Figures

Over time, these relational patterns create an unhealthy dynamic: the romantic partner **begins to resemble the over-involved parent**.

They may be expected to:

- Monitor the over-coddled individual's emotional state
- Provide constant validation
- Avoid conflict entirely
- Be available at all times
- Carry the mental load of both people

This not only burns out the partner, but it **prevents the over-coddled individual from growing**. They remain locked in an emotional childhood, unable to experience love as a partnership of two whole people—because they were never taught how to be whole on their own.

◈ What They Missed—and Can Still Learn

The good news? Emotional fragility is not fixed. With the right tools, awareness, and willingness to grow, even deeply dependent individuals can:

- Build emotional self-regulation
- Learn to communicate needs with clarity and respect
- Tolerate conflict without collapse
- Sit with discomfort without abandoning the relationship

But it requires **reversing the training** of over-coddling—by building the emotional muscles that were never exercised.

◈ Core Skills That Must Be Developed:

- **Emotional regulation**: Naming and managing emotions without requiring others to fix them
- **Boundary respect**: Understanding that space and difference are healthy
- **Conflict tolerance**: Learning that tension doesn't equal danger
- **Self-validation**: Feeling worthy without constant external affirmation

◈ Final Thoughts: Love Without Rescue

The most successful relationships are built on **two people who know how to take care of themselves—and choose to care for each other**. Over-coddled individuals were raised to believe love means rescue. But real love is about resilience, not dependency.

To truly thrive in relationships, they must learn that:

"It's not my partner's job to regulate my emotions. It's my job—and their support is a bonus, not a requirement."

Without this transformation, every relationship becomes another trap—one that looks like love but feels like panic.

Chapter 11: The School System's Role in Over-Coddling

When Educational Comfort Replaces Challenge—and Growth is the Cost

Over-coddling doesn't begin and end in the home. It extends into classrooms, cafeterias, counseling offices, and school policies that—though well-intentioned—have gradually shifted from **preparing children for life** to **protecting them from it.** In recent years, schools have increasingly embraced approaches that shield students from failure, challenge, and discomfort in the name of equity, emotional safety, or self-esteem. While some of these changes have offered needed reforms, many have had **unintended consequences**—especially when paired with over-coddling at home.

This chapter explores how **modern education has become another contributor to emotional fragility and dependency**, reinforcing the same patterns that create the Boomerang Generation. From **trigger warnings** to **grade inflation**, **no-zero policies**, and the **overuse of accommodations**, we'll examine how **protection has gone too far**—and what educators, parents, and administrators can do to help rebuild resilience in the classroom.

◈ **Participation Trophies and the Culture of Unconditional Reward**

The foundation for educational over-coddling often begins in early childhood education—where every child gets a sticker, a ribbon, or a trophy **just for showing up.**

On the surface, these practices aim to:

- Boost confidence
- Promote inclusivity
- Avoid discouragement

But beneath the surface, these habits often **strip achievements of meaning** and teach children that:

- **Effort and outcome are disconnected**
- **Mediocrity is celebrated**
- **There is no such thing as falling short**

Over time, this undermines **intrinsic motivation** and encourages an external reward mentality:

"I showed up, so where's my reward?"

"Why did someone else get more praise than I did?"

By removing the natural consequences of underperformance, schools **disincentivize effort** and weaken the connection between work and reward.

◈ Grade Inflation and No-Zero Policies: The End of Academic Accountability

To protect students from feeling defeated, many school districts have adopted **grade inflation practices** and **no-zero policies**, where students are given minimum grades regardless of effort—or lack thereof.

Examples of over-accommodation include:

- Giving a 50% grade for missing or incomplete work
- Allowing unlimited test retakes without meaningful feedback
- Eliminating deadlines entirely
- Capping the weight of final exams to prevent large grade drops
- Passing students regardless of literacy or numeracy skill level

While these policies often stem from a desire to keep students engaged, they **blur the lines between compassion and enabling**.

The result? Students who:

- Expect multiple chances with no accountability
- Put off work, knowing there's no consequence
- Don't build time management or planning skills
- Feel entitled to passing grades, even with poor performance
- Collapse in post-secondary environments where such accommodations are absent

By removing the possibility of failure, schools are also removing the **opportunity to develop persistence, self-reflection, and grit**—key ingredients of lifelong learning.

◈ Trigger Warnings and Emotional Over-Accommodation

In efforts to create safe spaces and trauma-informed environments, many educators have adopted the use of **trigger warnings**, emotional opt-outs, and hyper-sensitivity to discomfort.

Examples of emotional over-accommodation:

- Letting students skip assignments that deal with difficult topics
- Avoiding certain historical or literary subjects entirely
- Providing "safe spaces" during classroom discussions
- Reducing workload if a student is "emotionally distressed"

While the intention is often empathetic, these accommodations sometimes **reinforce the idea that discomfort is dangerous**, and that students should be protected from—not equipped to handle—intellectual and emotional challenges.

This undermines a child's capacity to:

- **Engage with complexity**
- **Navigate difficult emotions**
- **Build tolerance for opposing viewpoints**
- **Develop resilience in uncomfortable situations**

When children are allowed to disengage from anything distressing, they miss the developmental opportunity to practice **working through discomfort**, not around it.

◈◈ How Educators Unintentionally Foster Dependency

Teachers, counselors, and administrators often operate from a place of compassion—but sometimes that compassion becomes **counterproductive**.

Without realizing it, educators may:

- **Over-remind** students about deadlines, tests, or assignments
- **Negotiate every rule**, undermining consistency
- **Excuse behavior** instead of addressing it
- **Over-involve parents** in academic struggles, removing the student's responsibility
- **Allow technology (like AI or autocorrect tools)** to replace actual skill-building

These practices condition students to believe that:

- **Someone else will manage their time**
- **Rules are flexible based on emotional state**
- **Consequences can be negotiated away**
- **Parents or teachers will rescue them when things get hard**

In doing so, schools replicate the same **dependency cycle seen in over-coddling homes**, and children never learn to own their choices, cope with struggle, or recover from failure.

◈ **When Protection Goes Too Far: The Psychological Backlash**

Ironically, all this protection and accommodation—meant to support well-being—often leads to **greater anxiety, lower resilience, and poorer mental health**.

Psychological consequences include:

- **Anxiety over making mistakes**
- **Low tolerance for criticism or correction**
- **Difficulty adapting to structure**
- **Passive learning styles** (waiting to be told exactly what to do)
- **Overwhelm in unstructured or demanding environments**

In many cases, students excel within the scaffolded environment of school—then **collapse in college, work, or life**, where no one is curating their experience. Like over-watered plants, they've never learned how to stand upright without constant support.

◈ **A Systemic Issue: Not Just Individual but Institutional**

When entire school systems adopt over-coddling practices:

- Students graduate with **academic credentials but little functional confidence**
- Teachers burn out from over-managing behaviors and emotions
- Parents are conditioned to "step in" rather than step back
- Society sees a rising number of adults who **lack initiative, accountability, and emotional maturity**

This isn't a matter of soft-hearted teachers or weak students. It's a structural pattern that reflects deeper cultural fears—**fear of failure, fear of trauma, fear of not being enough**—and our attempt to preempt all pain instead of helping students grow through it.

◈ Solutions: Rebuilding Resilience in the Classroom

The goal of education should be to **equip, not protect.** Schools must find a new balance between empathy and accountability, between support and challenge.

What Schools Can Do:

- Reinstate meaningful **consequences for missed work**
- Offer **structured second chances**, not unlimited redos
- Use **natural consequences** instead of emotional cushioning
- Frame challenges as opportunities for growth, not trauma
- Encourage **open dialogue** rather than avoidance around tough topics
- Teach emotional regulation, not emotional avoidance

What Parents Can Do:

- Let children take responsibility for school communication
- Avoid rescuing them from academic consequences
- Support study habits and organization—but don't manage them entirely
- Reinforce the idea that **failure is a step toward mastery**

◈ Final Thoughts: Educating for Adulthood, Not Just Graduation

When we over-coddle in the classroom, we **graduate students who are intellectually capable but emotionally underdeveloped**. We equip them with facts but not fortitude. With grades but not grit.

True education is not about protecting children from challenge. It's about teaching them how to meet it with skill, confidence, and courage.

Chapter 12: Emotional Over-Control and Identity Suppression

When Safety Silences the Self

Adolescence is a critical time of self-discovery—a developmental crossroads when young people begin to ask the most important questions of their lives:

Who am I? What do I believe? What do I like? What matters to me?

This is the period where identity is meant to **unfold, clash, evolve, and emerge**. But for over-coddled children, this process often doesn't happen. Or worse, it happens in secret, guilt-ridden silence. When caregivers exert **emotional over-control**, dictating how children should feel, think, act, and relate, they don't just manage behavior—they suppress identity.

In this chapter, we'll explore how **micromanaging a child's emotions, interests, and relationships stifles identity formation**, especially in adolescence. You'll see how the pursuit of safety—emotional, social, or otherwise—can become so intense that it **smothers the child's authentic self**. And you'll discover why so many over-coddled teens grow into adults who **don't know who they are—because they've never had the chance to choose.**

◈ **What Is Emotional Over-Control?**

Emotional over-control happens when a caregiver:

- Monitors or dictates the child's feelings ("Don't be sad," "There's nothing to be afraid of")
- Intervenes in emotional expression ("That's enough crying")
- Redirects authentic emotion into "approved" feelings ("You're not angry, you're just tired")
- Controls social choices based on their own emotional comfort ("I don't like that friend—don't hang out with them")
- Rewards compliance and punishes emotional independence

Unlike overt abuse or neglect, emotional over-control can seem **loving or protective on the surface**. But at its core, it teaches the child:

"Your emotions, choices, and preferences are too risky to be trusted."

Over time, the child internalizes this message and begins to **filter or erase their emotional truth** to maintain peace or approval.

◈ **Micromanaging Feelings, Interests, and Friendships**

Parents and caregivers who micromanage often do so from fear—fear of the world, fear of poor influences, fear of their child getting hurt. But that fear can lead to **constant intervention** in areas where independence is essential:

1. Emotions

- Children aren't allowed to be upset, angry, anxious, or moody.
- Emotional expression is corrected rather than accepted.
- Caregivers step in to **resolve emotions**, rather than letting them be felt and processed.

2. Interests

- Choices about hobbies, music, clothing, or goals are **guided by what's safe, productive, or acceptable** to the parent.
- Children abandon genuine interests to please their caregivers.
- Creativity and curiosity are stifled in favor of compliance.

3. Friendships

- Parents approve or veto friendships based on perceived safety, class, race, religion, behavior, or influence.
- Children may hide friendships, feel ashamed of their peers, or avoid forming deep connections out of guilt or fear of rejection.
- The message becomes: *"You don't know what's good for you—I do."*

In each case, the child's **emerging identity is edited or overwritten** by parental control, resulting in **shame, confusion, and internal conflict.**

◈ The Adolescent Need for Autonomy and Exploration

Adolescence is a natural time of **pushback**—when children begin to question family values, assert preferences, and seek identity through trial and error.

This isn't rebellion. It's **healthy development**.

But emotional over-control sends the message that:

- Individuality is dangerous
- Autonomy is disloyal
- Dissent is disrespect

As a result, many over-coddled teens:

- **Suppress their opinions** to avoid confrontation
- **Seek secret autonomy**, hiding their true interests or choices
- **Feel lost or hollow**, unsure of who they really are
- **Fear disappointing their caregivers**, even at the cost of their own authenticity

This suppresses a vital psychological task: **identity formation**—the process by which teens explore, challenge, and define themselves.

When that task is interrupted or discouraged, the consequences stretch far beyond high school.

◈ The Cost of Always Being "Safe"

Safety is essential. But when safety becomes the **primary parenting goal**, it often comes at the expense of growth, creativity, and self-knowledge.

The emotional cost:

- **Low self-awareness**: Teens struggle to describe what they feel, want, or believe.
- **External locus of identity**: They define themselves through others' expectations.
- **Difficulty making decisions**: They lack practice in choosing based on inner truth.
- **Delayed individuation**: They remain emotionally fused with their parents into adulthood.

And when these young people do leave home, they may find themselves:

- Choosing college majors, jobs, or partners to **please their parents**
- Feeling like they're living **someone else's life**
- Struggling to assert themselves in romantic or professional settings
- Crumbling in crisis, because they've never defined their own values or path

Ultimately, they become **emotionally dependent adults**—not just in logistics, but in identity.

◈ Who Am I Without My Parent's Voice?

This is the haunting question many over-coddled young adults ask themselves:

"Who am I without someone else telling me what to feel, think, or choose?"

Their lives have been curated—feelings filtered, risks avoided, preferences "optimized." But in the absence of parental guidance, they often feel:

- **Directionless**: They don't know what brings joy or meaning.
- **Indecisive**: They fear making the "wrong" choice.
- **Ashamed**: They may reject their authentic identity because it doesn't match family values.
- **Inauthentic**: They wear personas to fit expectations, not to express truth.

These patterns can persist for years—or even decades—unless conscious effort is made to reconnect with the **true self** that was never given space to grow.

◈ Reclaiming Identity Through Autonomy and Acceptance

Identity cannot be **assigned**. It must be **discovered**.

To support healthy identity development—especially in teens—parents, teachers, and mentors must learn to:

- **Validate emotions without managing them**: "It's okay to feel that way."
- **Allow exploration without judgment**: "Try it and see what you think."
- **Model curiosity, not control**: "Tell me more about why you like that."
- **Support decision-making**: "It's your choice—I trust you to figure it out."
- **Respect evolving values and ideas**: "We don't have to agree for me to love you."

For over-coddled young adults, healing begins with **permission to be themselves**, even if it's messy, different, or uncomfortable.

It may take therapy, journaling, mentorship, or solo travel—but the work of identity reclamation is always worth doing.

◈ Final Thoughts: Authenticity Over Approval

Children are not meant to be perfect. They're meant to be **real**.

They're meant to feel, to explore, to make mistakes, to change their minds.

They're meant to discover who they are—**not who we expect them to be**.

Emotional over-control may produce polite, high-performing children—but it doesn't produce **whole, confident adults**. The cost of always being "safe" is often a life of confusion, passivity, and inauthenticity.

Chapter 13: Building Resilience – The Antidote to Over-Coddling

From Emotional Control to Emotional Strength

If over-coddling is the gentle trap, then **resilience is the key that unlocks the cage**. Resilience is what allows children not only to survive adversity but to grow stronger from it. It's the ability to bend without breaking, to feel without drowning, and to fail without quitting.

In over-coddled environments, children are often protected from emotional discomfort—but in doing so, we rob them of the very experiences that would teach them how to manage it. Emotional over-control stifles the opportunity to build **emotional resilience**, leaving children fragile and dependent.

This chapter explores **what real resilience looks like in children**, how to foster it with compassion—not cruelty—and why **small challenges and earned success** are the most powerful medicine for emotional growth. You'll learn how to shift from **emotional control** to **emotional coaching**, helping children sit with hard feelings, tolerate discomfort, and recover from emotional pain—the very skills they'll need for a lifetime of growth and independence.

◈ What Real Resilience Looks Like in Children

Resilience is often misunderstood as toughness or stoicism. But true resilience isn't about never feeling pain—it's about knowing how to move through pain **without collapsing or retreating.**
Emotionally resilient children can:

- Feel strong emotions **without needing to escape them**
- **Delay gratification** in favor of long-term rewards
- Handle mistakes and setbacks **without shame or avoidance**
- Ask for help **without expecting rescue**
- Self-soothe and calm themselves **without adult intervention**
- Try again—even after failure

These children don't avoid hard things. They learn to **approach them with confidence and flexibility**, knowing that difficulty is a part of life, not the end of it.

◈ From Emotional Control to Emotional Resilience

In over-coddled homes, emotional expression is often monitored, redirected, or minimized. Children are taught to **avoid distress**, to rely on caregivers for emotional regulation, and to fear failure or discomfort.

The goal of parenting must shift from **controlling emotions** to **coaching through them**.

Emotional Control:

- "Don't cry."
- "There's nothing to be upset about."
- "Let me fix it for you."
- "You're too sensitive."

Emotional Resilience:

- "It's okay to feel upset—let's breathe together."
- "That was hard. What do you want to try next?"
- "I can't solve this for you, but I'm here while you figure it out."
- "Feelings aren't bad—they're messengers."

By **acknowledging emotions instead of erasing them**, we give children permission to **build endurance and emotional literacy**, rather than becoming overwhelmed or dependent when pain arises.

◈ How to Foster Resilience Without Neglect or Cruelty

Resilience doesn't require harshness—it requires **structured challenge and loving support**. Children don't need to be thrown into the deep end to learn to swim. But they do need to **feel the water, practice paddling, and know someone is beside them if they falter.**

1. Let Them Struggle—Safely

- Allow them to try tasks on their own before stepping in.
- Let them forget homework, lose games, or feel bored—without rushing to fix it.
- Treat these experiences as **normal, not emergencies**.

2. Praise Effort, Not Outcome

- Focus on persistence, problem-solving, and emotional regulation.
- "You kept trying even though you were frustrated," is more valuable than "You're so smart."

3. Model Resilience

- Share your own challenges and how you handle setbacks.
- Avoid perfectionism—show that adults also make mistakes, feel overwhelmed, and recover.

4. Teach Self-Regulation Tools

- Deep breathing, naming emotions, journaling, movement, and reframing thoughts.
- Encourage breaks, not avoidance.

5. Encourage Independent Decision-Making

- Let them choose clothes, snacks, activities, or strategies—even if they fail.
- Reflect afterward with open-ended questions:

"What worked?"
"What would you try differently next time?"

◈ The Power of Small Challenges and Earned Success

Resilience is like a muscle—it grows through **repetition, resistance, and rest**. One of the most effective ways to build it is through **small, age-appropriate challenges that children learn to navigate on their own.**

Examples of resilience-building challenges:

- Finishing a difficult puzzle without help
- Speaking up to a teacher when confused
- Resolving a friendship conflict independently
- Handling a "no" without a meltdown
- Taking responsibility for a forgotten assignment

Each time a child **tries, struggles, and succeeds (or recovers from failure)**, they earn something that no amount of praise can provide: **real, embodied confidence**.

Over time, these small wins stack up to form a sturdy identity:

"I can figure things out. I don't have to be perfect. I can bounce back."

◈ What Happens Without Resilience?

Without resilience, children become:

- **Emotionally avoidant**: Dodging any situation that might cause distress
- **Externally dependent**: Waiting for someone else to fix their mood, problem, or failure
- **Easily discouraged**: Giving up when things aren't easy or perfect
- **Conflict-averse**: Shutting down rather than speaking up
- **Unprepared for adulthood**: Because real life demands recovery, not just success

They may feel safe for a while—but the **world doesn't operate like a coddling caregiver**. It challenges. It rejects. It surprises. And without emotional resilience, young adults may feel **like they're drowning the moment they're asked to swim.**

◈ Resilience Is the Foundation of True Independence

While over-coddling teaches children that they must be **protected**, resilience teaches them that they can be **prepared**.

Prepared to fail.

Prepared to feel.

Prepared to grow.

Prepared to face life on its terms—not just when it's easy.

This doesn't mean we should stop comforting children or offering support. It means we must stop removing every challenge. Because the goal is not to raise children who never fall—it's to raise children who **know how to get back up.**

◈ Final Thoughts: Resilience Over Rescue

Over-coddling says: "You can't handle this—let me do it."

Resilient parenting says: "This is hard—and I know you can get through it."

Children don't need a life without struggle. They need the **tools to meet struggle with courage, flexibility, and faith in themselves.** That's what builds a flourishing future—and a child who grows into an adult who thrives.

Chapter 14: Teaching Emotional Endurance

Helping Children Sit With Discomfort Without Shutting Down

In a world that prizes convenience, comfort, and instant gratification, we've unintentionally raised a generation that believes emotional pain is something to be avoided at all costs. But emotions are not enemies—they are messengers. And just like the immune system needs exposure to germs to grow strong, the emotional system **needs exposure to discomfort** to grow resilient.

This chapter is about teaching **emotional endurance**—the ability to stay present with hard emotions without shutting down, acting out, or demanding instant relief. Emotional endurance is not something children are born with. It must be **modeled, taught, and practiced** over time. Without it, we raise children who are emotionally reactive, avoidant, or dependent on others to "fix" their feelings. With it, we raise children who **trust their own ability to feel, process, and move forward with calm confidence.**

You'll learn how to help children **name, manage, and tolerate difficult emotions**, why shielding them from emotional pain actually makes them more fragile, and how to create **age-appropriate opportunities for real-life emotional growth.**

◈ Why Emotional Pain Is Not the Problem

Children are wired to feel deeply. But somewhere along the way, we began treating emotional pain as something dangerous—a crisis to solve, a signal of failure, or a threat to self-worth.

This belief leads parents and educators to:

- Rush to cheer children up at the first sign of sadness.
- Distract them from anger or boredom instead of addressing it.
- Solve emotional conflicts before children can process them.
- Avoid emotionally challenging topics or experiences.

But when we do this, we inadvertently teach children that:

- Emotions are problems, not parts of life.
- They cannot handle their own internal states.
- Someone else must fix their discomfort immediately.

This creates children who **lack emotional endurance**—the ability to sit with hard feelings, metabolize them, and move through them without panic or avoidance.

◈ What Is Emotional Endurance?

Emotional endurance is the **psychological capacity to remain present with an uncomfortable emotion**—without escaping it, suppressing it, or acting destructively.

It's the internal strength that allows a child to:

- Feel sadness without needing to be distracted.
- Feel anger without lashing out.
- Feel fear without freezing or fleeing.
- Feel disappointment without giving up.
- Feel anxiety without collapsing into avoidance.

This isn't about "being tough." It's about being **emotionally agile**—able to feel and still function.

◈ Helping Children Name and Understand Emotions

The foundation of emotional endurance is **emotional literacy**—the ability to identify and name what's happening inside.

Instead of simply reacting ("I'm mad!" "I hate this!"), children need language that gives shape to their experience.

Tools for Naming Emotions:

- **Feelings charts** with faces and words
- Simple scripts: "I feel ___ because ___."
- Reflective listening:

"It sounds like you're feeling frustrated because your plan didn't work."
"You look like you're sad. Do you want to talk about it?"

Why It Matters:

- Naming emotions activates the **prefrontal cortex**, calming the brain's fear center (amygdala).
- It teaches children that emotions are **data**, not directives—they can be felt without being obeyed.

◈ Why Shielding from Pain Makes It Worse

When children are never allowed to feel emotional discomfort, several things happen:

- Their **emotional tolerance stays low**—minor challenges feel overwhelming.
- They grow dependent on **external soothing or distraction**.
- They believe negative emotions mean **something is wrong with them**.
- They develop **avoidance strategies**: quitting, blaming, numbing, withdrawing.

In essence, shielding children from pain **weakens their emotional muscles**.

Just like physical endurance grows from repeated stress and recovery, emotional endurance grows from **exposure to manageable emotional discomfort, paired with compassionate support**.

◈ How to Build Emotional Endurance—Step by Step

Teaching emotional endurance is not a one-time lesson. It's a daily practice that evolves with age.

1. Validate First, Solve Second

"It makes sense that you feel this way."
"I understand why this is hard."

Validation helps a child feel safe enough to face their feelings, rather than needing to flee or suppress them.

2. Create Micro-Moments of Discomfort

Let children:

- Lose at games without changing the rules.
- Wait patiently instead of being immediately entertained.
- Make mistakes and sit with the consequences.
- Navigate peer disagreements without adult rescue.

These small moments build **resilience and regulation**.

3. Teach Self-Soothing Skills

Help children learn how to calm themselves:

- Deep breathing or guided visualization
- Journaling or drawing
- Gentle movement (walks, stretching)
- Naming the emotion and choosing a strategy

Instead of removing pain, teach them **how to care for themselves during it**.

4. Model Emotional Endurance

Children watch how adults handle discomfort. Be transparent:

- "I'm feeling overwhelmed right now, so I'm taking a break to reset."
- "I was disappointed about something today, but I reminded myself it's okay to feel that way."

Your example becomes their blueprint.

◈ Age-Appropriate Exposure to Real Life's Ups and Downs

Toddlers (1–3):

- Label feelings: "You're mad because it's bedtime."
- Stay calm during tantrums—don't try to eliminate all distress.
- Let them make small choices and sit with minor frustration.

Early Childhood (4–7):

- Let them struggle with puzzles or tying shoes without jumping in.
- Normalize sadness, boredom, and jealousy.
- Use stories to discuss how characters deal with emotions.

Middle Childhood (8–12):

- Allow natural consequences (forgetting homework, losing privileges).
- Encourage reflection: "What can you do differently next time?"
- Use challenges to teach coping, not avoidance.

Adolescence (13–18):

- Respect emotional complexity—don't minimize pain.
- Encourage healthy emotional outlets (music, sports, journaling).
- Guide them in setting boundaries and managing peer pressure.
- Support them in making big decisions—with your input, not control.

◈ Emotional Endurance Is the Inner World's Armor

When children learn to sit with discomfort:

- They stop fearing their emotions.
- They stop outsourcing their regulation.
- They start developing true **confidence**, not surface-level calm.

They grow into adults who can:

- Handle rejection and keep trying.
- Endure breakups without self-destruction.
- Survive job stress without shutting down.
- Feel grief, rage, disappointment—and still move forward.

In a world filled with pressure, triggers, and complexity, **emotional endurance isn't a luxury. It's a survival skill.**

◈ Final Thoughts: Sitting with Storms to Build Strength

We cannot raise emotionally strong children by protecting them from every storm.

We raise strong children by **teaching them how to sit in the storm, feel the rain, and know it will pass.**

That's endurance. That's emotional strength. That's the antidote to fragility.

Chapter 15: Parenting with Purpose, Not Protection

From Control to Courage: Raising Children Who Flourish

Parenting in the modern world often feels like walking a tightrope between nurturing and overprotecting, supporting and overstepping, loving and letting go. The instinct to protect is powerful—and natural. But if the journey of this book has shown us anything, it's this: **protection without preparation creates fragility, not strength.**

The final chapter in this journey invites you to **reframe your role as a parent—not as a shield, but as a guide.** Not as a fixer, but as a coach. Not as a controller, but as a cultivator of growth. Parenting with purpose means letting go of the illusion that we can remove all pain from our child's path. Instead, it means **trusting them enough to face the world on their own terms—with roots deep enough to hold and wings strong enough to soar.**

◈ From Shield to Guide: Redefining the Parenting Role

In over-coddling, the parent often plays the role of **shield**—stepping in to remove every obstacle, fix every mistake, soothe every emotion, and preempt every failure. But in doing so, they prevent the child from ever discovering their own strength.

A parent-as-guide:

- Walks *with* the child, not *in front of* them
- Offers tools, not solutions
- Encourages effort, not perfection
- Allows natural consequences to do the teaching
- Listens with empathy but resists the urge to rescue

When we shift from **protective parenting** to **purposeful parenting**, we create the conditions for our children to develop resilience, autonomy, identity, and courage.

◈ Practical Tools for Stepping Back and Trusting Growth

Letting go of control is not passive—it is an **active choice** that requires awareness, intention, and consistency. Here are real, tangible ways to step back while still staying lovingly present.

1. Ask More Questions, Give Fewer Answers

"What do you think you should do?"
"What does your gut tell you?"
"How would you handle this if I weren't here?"
This fosters independent thinking and emotional intelligence.

2. Delay Intervention

Before stepping in, ask yourself:
Is this a crisis, or just discomfort?
Give space for the child to try, stumble, and learn—while remaining nearby to support, not solve.

3. Let Natural Consequences Teach

When a child forgets their homework or loses a toy, let the resulting discomfort become a **teaching moment**, not a moment for rescue.

4. Use "Coach Language"

Instead of directives ("Do this"), try language that empowers:
"You've got this."
"I trust you."
"It's okay to be unsure—start anyway."

5. Create a Household Culture of Growth

- Celebrate effort, not outcomes.
- Normalize failure.
- Share your own struggles and lessons.
- Set family goals around courage, patience, and grit—not just achievements.

◈ Letting Go of Control to Embrace Trust

For many parents, the hardest part of this journey is **letting go**—not of love, but of **ownership over the child's path**. Letting go means trusting:

- That your child will stumble—but stand again.
- That they may choose differently than you—but still be okay.
- That pain will come—but it won't destroy them.
- That you've planted enough seeds—and now they must grow.

This trust is the deepest form of love. It honors your child as a whole person—one who doesn't need to be molded, but supported as they unfold.

◈ **Preparing Your Child for a World That Won't Always Be Gentle**

The world your child is entering is **uncertain, fast-paced, emotionally complex**, and often unforgiving. You cannot remove its rough edges—but you can prepare your child to meet it with grace, grit, and groundedness.

What preparation looks like:

- Teaching them to *sit with discomfort* instead of escaping it.
- Giving them chances to *fail safely* and reflect.
- Equipping them with *emotional tools* for sadness, frustration, and fear.
- Trusting them to *make decisions and learn from them*.
- Encouraging curiosity over compliance, and growth over perfection.

They don't need perfection—they need **practice**. They don't need protection from every storm—they need to **learn how to stand in the wind.**

◈ Children With Strong Roots Don't Just Survive—They Flourish

Everything we've explored in this book has one central theme: **the power of intentional, courageous parenting.**

A child who is:

- Allowed to struggle...
- Encouraged to explore...
- Guided but not gripped...
- Loved for who they are, not who we expect them to be...

...will not only survive the challenges of life. They will **flourish in spite of them.**

They will:

- Lead with confidence.
- Connect with empathy.
- Fail with dignity.
- Rise with resilience.

They will not need rescuing—because they will **know how to rescue themselves.**

◈ Final Message: Parenting With Purpose Is a Gift You Give for Life

You cannot predict your child's future. But you can shape their **inner world**—a world built on strength, trust, adaptability, and self-awareness.

Parenting with purpose means:

- Loving without smothering.
- Guiding without gripping.
- Letting go without abandoning.

It means creating a legacy not of dependence, but of empowerment.

Because in the end, your child's greatest strength will not be that they were protected from every hardship. It will be that they **were prepared to face it, feel it, and grow because of it.**

Appendix A: Signs of Over-Coddling by Age Group

Checklist & Reflection Tool for Parents, Educators, and Caregivers

Over-coddling can be difficult to detect because it often masquerades as love, support, and attentiveness. But the line between **nurturing** and **over-managing** is thinner than most realize. This appendix provides a developmental breakdown of over-coddling patterns from toddlerhood through early adulthood, followed by reflective journal prompts to help you realign with purposeful parenting.

Remember: this tool is not about guilt or shame. It's about **awareness**—so you can adjust your parenting in ways that empower your child to grow into a strong, independent, and emotionally resilient adult.

◈ **Toddlers (Ages 1–3)**
◈ *Signs of Over-Coddling:*

- Frequently doing things for the child they are developmentally capable of trying (e.g., feeding, walking, choosing clothes).
- Preventing all frustration (e.g., switching toys before tantrums, never allowing "no").
- Constantly distracting the child from emotions rather than naming them (e.g., "Look over here!" instead of "You're sad because...").
- Rarely allowing independent exploration due to fear of injury or mess.
- Avoiding exposure to small discomforts like waiting, taking turns, or falling.

◈ *What's Needed Instead:*

- Gentle encouragement to try new things independently.
- Validation of emotions ("It's okay to feel mad") instead of suppression.
- Safe opportunities to problem-solve or experience delayed gratification.

◈ **Early Childhood (Ages 4–7)**
◈ *Signs of Over-Coddling:*

- Micromanaging every decision (what to wear, how to play, what to say).
- Intervening in every social conflict or peer disagreement.
- Giving excessive praise without effort ("You're amazing!" regardless of actual behavior).
- Completing their responsibilities "to save time" (e.g., making bed, packing bag).
- Avoiding all consequences for rule-breaking or mistakes.

◈ *What's Needed Instead:*

- Practice making simple decisions and experiencing natural outcomes.
- Guided conversations about emotions and conflict resolution.
- Chores and responsibilities to build competence and self-worth.

◈ Middle Childhood (Ages 8–12)
◈ *Signs of Over-Coddling:*

- Doing school projects, homework, or assignments for them.
- Constantly checking in or hovering at school or extracurriculars.
- Blaming teachers or peers for all disappointments or conflicts.
- Over-scheduling to prevent boredom or struggle.
- Refusing to allow them to experience "failure," and demanding changes in policy or grading.

◈ *What's Needed Instead:*

- Support with organization, but not takeover.
- Exposure to challenges, setbacks, and how to bounce back.
- Discussions about responsibility, fairness, and emotional management.

◈ **Adolescents (Ages 13–18)**
◈ *Signs of Over-Coddling:*

- Monitoring texts, calls, and personal relationships excessively.
- Making major decisions (college, extracurriculars) on their behalf.
- Calling teachers, coaches, or employers to resolve conflicts.
- Excusing lack of effort or accountability due to stress or emotions.
- Refusing to allow them to experience the consequences of risky or poor choices.

◈ *What's Needed Instead:*

- Honest, ongoing dialogue around autonomy and boundaries.
- Encouragement to self-advocate, plan ahead, and follow through.
- Respect for their growing identity—even when it differs from your own.

◈ **Young Adults (Ages 18–25)**
◈ *Signs of Over-Coddling:*

- Managing their schedules, finances, job searches, or academic responsibilities.
- Preventing them from moving out due to fear they "aren't ready."
- Intervening in adult relationships, workplace conflicts, or legal/financial issues.
- Providing comfort to the point of dependency (e.g., cooking, cleaning, driving everywhere).
- Pressuring them to make life decisions that reflect your comfort, not their growth.

◈ *What's Needed Instead:*

- A shift toward mutual adult boundaries and expectations.
- Emotional support paired with encouragement to problem-solve.
- Room for mistakes, responsibility, and identity development.

⬦ **Reflection Journal Prompts and Self-Assessment**

Use the prompts below to deepen your self-awareness and identify where adjustments might help you parent or support with more purpose and less protection.

⬦ *Weekly Reflection Questions:*

1. **Where did I step in today when I could have stepped back?**
2. **Did I offer comfort, or did I accidentally take over?**
3. **What difficult emotion did my child express that I tried to solve or minimize?**
4. **What decision did I make for my child that they were capable of making themselves?**
5. **Where did my fear of discomfort override their need for experience?**
6. **Did I praise effort or just outcome this week?**
7. **How often did I validate their feelings without trying to change them?**
8. **What's one area this week where I can practice letting go of control?**
9. **Have I asked my child what they want, think, or feel—or just assumed I know best?**
10. **Am I preparing them to live without me—or keeping them dependent on me?**

⬦ **Final Reminder:**

Parenting with purpose is not about getting everything right—it's about being **conscious, courageous, and willing to grow alongside your child.** It's not about never stepping in—it's about knowing **when to step back** so your child can step up.

Because in the end, your role is not to create a life without struggle, but to prepare a child who is strong enough to navigate it with **character, clarity, and confidence.**

<u>Message from the Author:</u>

I hope you enjoyed this book, I love astrology and knew there was not a book such as this out on the shelf. I love metaphysical items as well. Please check out my other books:

-Life of Government Benefits

-My life of Hell

-My life with Hydrocephalus

-Red Sky

-World Domination:Woman's rule

-World Domination:Woman's Rule 2: The War

-Life and Banishment of Apophis: book 1

-The Kidney Friendly Diet

-The Ultimate Hemp Cookbook

-Creating a Dispensary(legally)

-Cleanliness throughout life: the importance of showering from childhood to adulthood.

-Strong Roots: The Risks of Overcoddling children

-Hemp Horoscopes: Cosmic Insights and Earthly Healing

- Celestial Hemp Navigating the Zodiac: Through the Green Cosmos

-Astrological Hemp: Aligning The Stars with Earth's Ancient Herb

-The Astrological Guide to Hemp: Stars, Signs, and Sacred Leaves

-Green Growth: Innovative Marketing Strategies for your Hemp Products and Dispensary

-Cosmic Cannabis

-Astrological Munchies

-Henry The Hemp

-Zodiacal Roots: The Astrological Soul Of Hemp

- **Green Constellations: Intersection of Hemp and Zodiac**

-Hemp in The Houses: An astrological Adventure Through The Cannabis Galaxy

-Galactic Ganja Guide

Heavenly Hemp

Zodiac Leaves

Doctor Who Astrology

Cannastrology

Stellar Satvias and Cosmic Indicas

Celestial Cannabis: A Zodiac Journey

AstroHerbology: The Sky and The Soil: Volume 1

AstroHerbology:Celestial Cannabis:Volume 2

Cosmic Cannabis Cultivation

The Starry Guide to Herbal Harmony: Volume 1

The Starry Guide to Herbal Harmony: Cannabis Universe: Volume 2

Yugioh Astrology: Astrological Guide to Deck, Duels and more

Nightmare Mansion: Echoes of The Abyss

Nightmare Mansion 2: Legacy of Shadows

Nightmare Mansion 3: Shadows of the Forgotten

Nightmare Mansion 4: Echoes of the Damned

The Life and Banishment of Apophis: Book 2

Nightmare Mansion: Halls of Despair

Healing with Herb: Cannabis and Hydrocephalus

Planetary Pot: Aligning with Astrological Herbs: Volume 1

Fast Track to Freedom: 30 Days to Financial Independence Using AI, Assets, and Agile Hustles

Cosmic Hemp Pathways

How to Become Financially Free in 30 Days: 10,000 Paths to Prosperity

Zodiacal Herbage: Astrological Insights: Volume 1

Nightmare Mansion: Whispers in the Walls

The Daleks Invade Atlantis

Henry the hemp and Hydrocephalus

10X The Kidney Friendly Diet

Cannabis Universe: Adult coloring book

Hemp Astrology: The Healing Power of the Stars

Zodiacal Herbage: Astrological Insights: Cannabis Universe: Volume 2

<u>Planetary Pot: Aligning with Astrological Herbs: Cannabis Universes: Volume 2</u>

Doctor Who Meets the Replicators and SG-1: The Ultimate Battle for Survival

Nightmare Mansion: Curse of the Blood Moon

<u>The Celestial Stoner: A Guide to the Zodiac</u>

Cosmic Pleasures: Sex Toy Astrology for Every Sign

Hydrocephalus Astrology: Navigating the Stars and Healing Waters

Lapis and the Mischievous Chocolate Bar

Celestial Positions: Sexual Astrology for Every Sign

Apophis's Shadow Work Journal: **:** A Journey of Self-Discovery and Healing

Kinky Cosmos: Sexual Kink Astrology for Every Sign

Digital Cosmos: The Astrological Digimon Compendium

Stellar Seeds: The Cosmic Guide to Growing with Astrology

Apophis's Daily Gratitude Journal

Cat Astrology: Feline Mysteries of the Cosmos

The Cosmic Kama Sutra: An Astrological Guide to Sexual Positions

Unleash Your Potential: A Guided Journal Powered by AI Insights

Whispers of the Enchanted Grove

Cosmic Pleasures: An Astrological Guide to Sexual Kinks

369, 12 Manifestation Journal

Whisper of the nocturne journal(blank journal for writing or drawing)

The Boogey Book

Locked In Reflection: A Chastity Journey Through Locktober

Generating Wealth Quickly:How to Generate $100,000 in 24 Hours

Star Magic: Harness the Power of the Universe

The Flatulence Chronicles: A Fart Journal for Self-Discovery

The Doctor and The Death Moth

Seize the Day: A Personal Seizure Tracking Journal

The Ultimate Boogeyman Safari: A Journey into the Boogie World and Beyond

Whispers of Samhain: 1,000 Spells of Love, Luck, and Lunar Magic: Samhain Spell Book

Apophis's guides:Witch's Spellbook Crafting Guide for Halloween

<u>Frost & Flame: The Enchanted Yule Grimoire of 1000 Winter Spells</u>

<u>The Ultimate Boogey Goo Guide & Spooky Activities for Halloween Fun</u>

Harmony of the Scales: A Libra's Spellcraft for Balance and Beauty

The Enchanted Advent: 36 Days of Christmas Wonders

Nightmare Mansion: The Labyrinth of Screams

Harvest of Enchantment: 1,000 Spells of Gratitude, Love, and Fortune for Thanksgiving

The Boogey Chronicles: A Journal of Nightly Encounters and Shadowy Secrets

The 12 Days of Financial Freedom: A Step-by-Step Christmas Countdown to Transform Your Finances

Sigil of the Eternal Spiral Blank Journal

A Christmas Feast: Timeless Recipes for Every Meal

Holiday Stress-Free Solutions: A Survival Guide to Thriving During the Festive Season

Yu-Gi-Oh! Holiday Gifting Mastery: The Ultimate Guide for Fans and Newcomers Alike

Holiday Harmony: A Hydrocephalus Survival Guide for the Festive Season

Celestial Craft: The Witch's Almanac for 2025 – A Cosmic Guide to Manifestations, Moons, and Mystical Events

Doctor Who: The Toymaker's Winter Wonderland

Tulsa King Unveiled: A Thrilling Guide to Stallone's Mafia Masterpiece

Pendulum Craft: A Complete Guide to Crafting and Using Personalized Divination Tools

Nightmare Mansion: Santa's Eternal Eve

Starlight Noel: A Cosmic Journey through Christmas Mysteries

The Dark Architect: Unlocking the Blueprint of Existence

Surviving the Embrace: The Ultimate Guide to Encounters with The Hugging Molly

The Enchanted Codex: Secrets of the Craft for Witches, Wiccans, and Pagans

Harvest of Gratitude: A Complete Thanksgiving Guide

Yuletide Essentials: A Complete Guide to an Authentic and Magical Christmas

Celestial Smokes: A Cosmic Guide to Cigars and Astrology

Living in Balance: A Comprehensive Survival Guide to Thriving with Diabetes Insipidus

Cosmic Symbiosis: The Venom Zodiac Chronicles

The Cursed Paw of Ambition

Cosmic Symbiosis: The Astrological Venom Journal

Celestial Wonders Unfold: A Stargazer's Guide to the Cosmos (2024-2029)

The Ultimate Black Friday Prepper's Guide: Mastering Shopping Strategies and Savings

Cosmic Sales: The Astrological Guide to Black Friday Shopping

Legends of the Corn Mother and Other Harvest Myths

Whispers of the Harvest: The Corn Mother's Journal

The Evergreen Spellbook

The Doctor Meets the Boogeyman

The White Witch of Rose Hall's SpellBook

The Gingerbread Golem's Shadow: A Study in Sweet Darkness

The Gingerbread Golem Codex: An Academic Exploration of Sweet Myths

The Gingerbread Golem Grimoire: Sweet Magicks and Spells for the Festive Witch

The Curse of the Gingerbread Golem

10-minute Christmas Crafts for kids

<u>Christmas Crisis Solutions: The Ultimate Last-Minute Survival Guide</u>

Gingerbread Golem Recipes: Holiday Treats with a Magical Twist

The Infinite Key: Unlocking Mystical Secrets of the Ages

Enchanted Yule: A Wiccan and Pagan Guide to a Magical and Memorable Season

Dinosaurs of Power: Unlocking Ancient Magick

Astro-Dinos: The Cosmic Guide to Prehistoric Wisdom

Gallifrey's Yule Logs: A Festive Doctor Who Cookbook

The Dino Grimoire: Secrets of Prehistoric Magick

The Gift They Never Knew They Needed

The Gingerbread Golem's Culinary Alchemy: Enchanting Recipes for a Sweetly Dark Feast

A Time Lord Christmas: Holiday Adventures with the Doctor

Krampusproofing Your Home: Defensive Strategies for Yule

Silent Frights: A Collection of Christmas Creepypastas to Chill Your Bones

Santa Raptor's Jolly Carnage: A Dino-Claus Christmas Tale

Prehistoric Palettes: A Dino Wicca Coloring Journey

The Christmas Wishkeeper Chronicles

The Starlight Sleigh: A Holiday Journey

Elf Secrets: The True Magic of the North Pole

Candy Cane Conjurations

Cooking with Kids: Recipes Under 20 Minutes

Doctor Who: The TARDIS Confiscation

The Anxiety First Aid Kit: Quick Tools to Calm Your Mind

Frosty Whispers: A Winter's Tale

The Infinite Key: Unlocking the Secrets to Prosperity, Resilience, and Purpose

The Grasping Void: Why You'll Regret This Purchase

Astrology for Busy Bees: Star Signs Simplified

The Instant Focus Formula: Cut Through the Noise

The Secret Language of Colors: Unlocking the Emotional Codes

Sacred Fossil Chronicles: Blank Journal

The Christmas Cottage Miracle

Feeding Frenzy: Graboid-Inspired Recipes

Manifest in Minutes: The Quick Law of Attraction Guide

The Symbiote Chronicles: Doctor Who's Venomous Journey

Think Tiny, Grow Big: The Minimalist Mindset

The Energy Key: Unlocking Limitless Motivation

New Year, New Magic: Manifesting Your Best Year Yet

Unstoppable You: Mastering Confidence in Minutes

Infinite Energy: The Secret to Never Feeling Drained

Lightning Focus: Mastering the Art of Productivity in a Distracted World

Saturnalia Manifestation Magick: A Guide to Unlocking Abundance During the Solstice

Graboids and Garland: The Ultimate Tremors-Themed Christmas Guide

12 Nights of Holiday Magic

The Power of Pause: 60-Second Mindfulness Practices

The Quick Reset: How to Reclaim Your Life After Burnout

The Shadow Eater: A Tale of Despair and Survival

The Micro-Mastery Method: Transform Your Skills in Just Minutes a Day

Reclaiming Time: How to Live More by Doing Less

Chronovore: The Eternal Nexus

The Mind Reset: Unlocking Your Inner Peace in a Chaotic World

Confidence Code: Building Unshakable Self-Belief

Baby the Vampire Terrier

Baby the Vampire Terrier's Christmas Adventure

Celestial Streams: The Content Creator's Astrology Manual

The Wealth Whisperer: Unlocking Abundance with Everyday Actions

The Energy Equation: Maximize Your Output Without Burning Out

The Happiness Algorithm: Science-Backed Steps to Joyful Living

Stress-Free Success: Achieving Goals Without Anxiety

Mindful Wealth: The New Blueprint for Financial Freedom

The Festive Flavors of New Year: A Culinary Celebration

The Master's Gambit: Keys of Eternal Power

Shadowed Secrets: Groundhog Day Mysteries

Beneath the Burrow: Lessons from the Groundhog

Spring's Whispers: The Groundhog's Prediction

The Limitless Mindset: Unlock Your Untapped Potential

The Focus Funnel: How to Cut Through Chaos and Get Results

Bold Moves: Building Courage to Live on Your Terms

The Daily Shift: Simple Practices for Lasting Transformation

The Quarter-Life Reset: Thriving in Your 20s and 30s

The Art of Shadowplay: Building Your Own Personal Myth

The Eternal Loop: Finding Purpose in Repetition

Burrowing Wisdom: Life Lessons from the Groundhog

Shadow Work: A Groundhog Day Perspective

Love in Bloom: 5-Minute Romantic Gestures

The Shadowspell Codex: Secrets of Forbidden Magick

The Burnout Cure: Finding Balance in a Busy World

The Groundhog Prophecy: Unlocking Seasonal Secrets

Nog Tales: The Spirited History of Eggnog

Six More Weeks: Embracing Seasonal Transitions
The Lumivian Chronicles: Fragments of the Fifth Dimension
Money on Your Mind: A Beginner's Guide to Wealth
The Focus Fix: Breaking Through Distraction
January's Spirit Keepers: Mystical Protectors of the Cold
Creativity Unchained: Unlocking Your Wildest Ideas in 2025
Manifestation Mastery: 365 Days to Rewrite Your Reality
The Groundhog's Mirror: Reflecting on Change
The Weeping Angels' Christmas Curse
Burrowed in Time: A Groundhog Day Journey
Heartbeats: Poems to Share with Your Valentine
Dino Wicca: The Sacred Grimoire of Prehistoric Magick
Courage of the Pride: Finding Your Inner Roar
The Lion's Leap: Bold Moves for Big Results
Healthy Hustle: Achieving Without Overworking
Practical Manifesting: Turning Dreams into Reality in 2025
Jurassic Pharaohs: Unlocking the Magick of Ancient Egypt and Dino Wicca
The Happiness Equation: Small Changes for Big Joy
The Confidence Compass: Finding Your Inner Strength
Whispers in the Hollow: Tales of the Forgotten Beasts
Echoes from the Hollow: The Return of Forgotten Beasts
The Hollow Ascendant: The Rise of the Forgotten Beasts
The Relationship Reset: Building Better Connections
Mastering the Morning: How to Win the Day Before 8 AM
The Shadow's Dance: Groundhog Day Symbolism
Cupid's Kitchen: Quick Valentine's Day Recipes
Valentine's Day on a Budget: Love Without Breaking the Bank
Astrocraft: Aligning the Stars in the World of Minecraft
Forecasting Life: Groundhog Day Reflections
Bleeding Hearts: Twisted Tales of Valentine's Terror
Herbal Smoke Revolution: The Ultimate Guide to Nature's Cigarette Alternative

Winter's Wrath: The Complete Survival Blueprint for Extreme Freezes.

The Groundhog's Shadow: A Tale of Seasons

Burrowed Insights: Wisdom from the Groundhog

Sensual Strings: The Art of Erotic Bondage

Whispered Flames: Unlocking the Power of Fire Play

Forgotten Shadows: A Guide to Cryptids Lost to Time

Six Weeks of Secrets: Groundhog Day's Hidden Messages

Shadows and Cycles: Groundhog Day Reflections

The Art of Love Letters: Crafting the Perfect Message

Romantic Getaways at Home: Turning Your Space into Paradise

Purrfect Brews: A Cat Lover's Guide to Coffee and Companionship

The Groundhog's Wisdom: Timeless Lessons for Modern Life

The Shadow Oracle: Groundhog Day as a Predictor

Emerging from the Burrow: A Journey of Renewal

The Language of Love: Learning Your Partner's Love Style

Authorpreneur: The Ultimate Blueprint for Writing, Publishing, and Thriving as an Author

Weathering the Seasons: Groundhog Day Perspectives

Valentine's Day Magic: A Guide to Romantic Rituals

The Shadow Chronicles: Stories of Groundhog Day

Love and Laughter: Fun Games for Valentine's Day

AstroRealty: Unlocking the Stars for Property Success

The Groundhog's Path: A Guide to Seasonal Balance

Groundhog Day Diaries: Reflections in the Shadow

The Groundhog's Light: Illuminating the Path Ahead

Valentine's Traditions from Around the World

AI Wealth Revolution: Unlocking the Trillionaire Mindset

Love Rekindled: Reigniting Passion in Relationships

Single and Thriving: Self-Love on Valentine's Day

Emerald Legends: Mystical Tales of Ireland

Green Alchemy: Harnessing Nature's Magic

The Hearts of Horror: A Valentine's Day Nightmare

The Leprechaun's Guide to Wealth and Wisdom

Dancing with the Sidhe: Celebrating the Otherworld

Shamrocks and Shadows: Mysteries of the Green Isle

Emerald Energy: Harnessing Luck and Growth

The Gingerbread Golem's Valentine: A Sweetheart's Guide to Love and Enchantment

The Celtic Knot: Weaving Life and Destiny

Green Fire: Elemental Magic for St. Patrick's Day

Clover Chronicles: Finding Your Inner Luck

Ireland's Mystical Creatures: A Field Guide

Gingerbread Golem's Love Almanac

Prowl and Thrive: The Lion's Guide to Success

Love Alchemy: Transforming Your Life Through Heart Energy

WORLD DOMINATION: Woman's Rule 3:The New Life

The Midnight Rose: A Guide to Lunar Love Spells

The Forbidden Letters: Writing Your Own Love Prophecy

Luck and Lore: St. Patrick's Day for Modern Mystics

The Green Path: A Pagan Celebration of Renewal

The Dark Architect's Guide to Reprogramming Reality

Prankster's Paradise: A Guide to Harmless Hijinks

Manifest Your Reality: The Law of Attraction Simplified

The TARDIS Owner's Manual: Understanding the Doctor's Ship: *A complete guide to the TARDIS, its technology, secrets, and mysteries*

Starlit Romance: Astrology Secrets for Finding True Love

The Time Lord's Atlas: A Complete Guide to the Whoniverse: *A breakdown of the locations, planets, and dimensions explored in Doctor Who*

Sweetheart Shadows: The Dark Side of Love and Attraction

February Fire: Reigniting Passion in Every Area of Life

The Self-Love Toolkit: 5 Ways to Embrace Who You Are
February Sparks: Ignite Your Dreams in 28 Days
March to Success: A 31-Day Action Blueprint
Ancient Paths: The 13 Sacred Principles of Dino Wicca
Echoes of Tomorrow: Navigating the AI Revolution
The Wellness Blueprint: Balancing Mind, Body, and Soul
Green Horizons: Sustainable Living for a Better Tomorrow
The AI Wealth Code: How to Make Millions with Automation
AI-Powered Creativity: Writing, Art, and Music for Profit
Extinction Rites: Rebirthing Your Soul Through Prehistoric Magick
Sacred Serpents tarot
Celestial Enchantment blank journal
Star Strains
Culinary Journeys: Exploring Global Flavors at Home
The Hollowvale Curse
The Hollowvale Harvest
The Egg of Transformation: Awakening Your Inner Power
Blooming Into Power: A Wiccan Guide to Spring Awakening
The Nightmare Nexus: The Third Doctor's Perilous Haunting
Digital Detox: Reclaiming Your Life in a Connected World
Ostara's Path: Walking the Spiral of Renewal
The Sacred Hare
Financial Freedom: Building Wealth in the Modern Age
Spring's Cauldron: Stirring the Waters of Change
The Hollowvale Pact
Quantum Consciousness: The Science of Reality Shifting
The Hollowvale Hunger
The Sacred Waters Within: A Witch's Guide to Hydrocephalus Magick
The Raven's Nest: Building a Life of Unshakable Stability
AI and the Human Mind: The Future of Intelligence
The Hollowvale Reckoning

Timeless Love: Building and Maintaining Lasting Relationships

The Raven's Roar: Unlocking Unstoppable Confidence

Raven Sight: Awakening Intuition and Inner Wisdom

The Butterfly Effect: Small Changes, Big Transformations

Taming the Boogeyman: How to Conquer Your Inner Fears

The Magick of Green: Awakening Earth's Energy in You

The Entrepreneurial Mindset: Secrets to Business Success

The Hollowvale End

The Shadow Luck Ritual: Reclaiming Power from Your Dark Side

Spring Magick for Beginners: A Simple Guide to Seasonal Energy Work

Doctor Who: The Hollowvale Conundrum

The March of Miracles: Unlocking Synchronicities in Spring

Unveiling the Cosmos: A Guide to Stargazing and Space Exploration

The Ultimate Guide to Surviving an Economic Collapse

The AI Gold Rush: How to Profit from the AI Revolution

Bastet's Shadow: The Hidden Power of Feline Magick

The Bastet Codex: Unlocking the Goddess's Magickal Secrets

Purring Spells: Harnessing Bastet's Healing Frequencies

Bastet's Nine Lives: Rebirth, Transformation, and Immortality Spells

Primal Currents: Hydrocephalus Magick in the Path of Dino Wicca

The Digital Gold Rush: Mastering E-Commerce and Online Sales

Future Shock: Adapting to the Next Decade of Change

The Quantum Mindset: Think Like a Billionaire

Sacred Motherhood: Awakening the Divine Feminine Within

The Mother's Spellbook: Enchantments for Love, Protection, and Prosperity

The Witch's Guide to Parenting: Raising Empowered and Intuitive Children

The Magick of Motherhood: Reclaiming Your Power Through Rituals

The Pagan Path to Self-Love: A Goddess's Guide to Worth and Confidence

Wild Woman Magick: Unleashing Your Primal Power

The Money Magnet Blueprint: Unlocking Unlimited Wealth

Biohacking 101: Unlock Your Body's Full Potential

The Wild Father: A Pagan Guide to Strength and Wisdom

The Sacred Masculine: Unlocking Your Inner Power

The Druid's Compass

The Warrior's Mindset

The Father's Fire

Odin's Path

Ancestral Bonds

The House That Whispers

The Magician's Code

The Wild Hunt

The Green Man's Path

The Altar of Success

The Shadow and the Sword

The High Priestess's Guide to Energy Healing

The Lunar Mother

The Sacred Self-Care Grimoire

The Womb Wisdom Codex

The Wheel of the Mother

The Witch's Guide to Manifestation

The Q2 Reset

The Ultimate Guide to AI-Powered Passive Income

Escape the 9-5

AI Feline Fortunes

The Tear-Stained Grimoire

Razorblade Runes
Cemetery Sirens
The Midnight Wristwatch
The Town That Forgets
AI Horror & Creepypasta
The Hollow Frequency
The Breach Echo
The Quiet Between Worlds
The Sigil of Tharan-Khul
Summon the Vault of Y'ha'ten
The Becoming Codex
The Profit of Az'ra-nar
The Drowned Logos
Echoes of the Eldritch Will
The Deep Ledger
Necronomicon of Networth
Covenant of the Wealthwyrm
The Whisperer's Manifesto
The Rites of Azh-K'luth
The Ark of the Crawling Coin
The Tithe of Shadows
Inkheart Abyss
The Timewinds of Y'ha-nthlei
The Spiral Labyrinth of Azag-Nirrh
The Gallifreyan Heresy of the Black Pharaoh
The Psalms of Nyog-Sotha
Black Rain Alchemy
The Infinite Maw
The Entropic Blueprint
The Oracle of Sh'guul
The Book of Breach
The Drowned Saint's Testament
Dreamcraft of the Sleeper God

The Silence Market
Cthonomics: The Dark Wealth Algorithm
Invocation of the Ten-Eyed King
Wealthbound to the Wyrm Below
Become the Unnameable
Codex of the Sovereign Flame
Rituals of Relentless Becoming
The Shadow Ascends
The Eyes Beneath You
The Will That Wakes Worlds
Silence Is a Weapon
The Mirror That Screams
The Whisper Between Moments
The Mind That Devours Fear
The Myth of the Finished Self
The Architect of Your Madness
The Voice You've Buried
The Discipline of Madness
Stormborn: Awakening Your Inner Tempest
The Mind That Ate Time
Unbind Your Becoming
The Pact You Owe Yourself
The Devourer's Diet
The Acid That Carves the Path
The Tower You Must Burn
The Breath Between Worlds
Speak Like the Deep
The Labyrinth Within
The Spine of the Sea God
Rejection Is a Portal
The Crown You Refused
The Scar Is the Spell
The Lightless Flame

The Habit of Becoming Horrific

ChickenJockey Chaos

The Gatekeeper Within

You Are Not Your Name

The Compass of the Mad

The Archive of Unsent Letters

What the Mirror Can't Show You

The Knife You Needed

Worship Nothing, Become Everything

The Other Voice

The Body the World Forgot

The Vein of the Void

The Black Bone Codex

The Puzzle of the Hidden Self (Millennium Puzzle)

The Eye That Sees the Lie *(Millennium Eye)*

The Ring of Return (Millennium Ring)

The Rod of Relentless Will *(Millennium Rod)*

The Tally of the Soul (Millennium Tauk/Necklace)

The Key to the Locked Timeline (Millennium Key)

The Scale of Sacred Decisions (Millennium Scales)

Inferno Bites: The UnOfficial Minecraft Lava Cookbook

Rot in the Attic

Prana: The Hidden Force of Your Infinite Self

The Shadow Realm Within: Transforming Darkness Into Destiny

The Borderland Collapse

Claws of Protection: Bastet's Defensive Magick

Mr. Ring-a-Ding's Madness

Yugioh Astrology: Celestial Deckcraft and Duel Destiny (2026–2027 Edition)

The Seal You Signed: Unlocking the Power You Once Feared

The Puzzle of Infinite Minds: Unlocking the Mentalism Hidden Within

The Eye That Mirrors the All: Secrets of Inner Reflection
Doctor Who: The Toymaker's Broadcast
The Rod of Eternal Flow: Commanding the Currents of Vibration
Golden Eyes of Bastet: Enhancing Psychic Vision
The Key of Dual Forces: Balance Within the Polarity
The Scales of Living Rhythm: Timing the Dance of Life
The Necklace of Hidden Cause: Weaving the Webs of Fate
The Ring of Secret Masters: Rising Through the All Within All
Daggers of the Dying Deep
Bastet's Wealth and Fortune Magick: Prosperity Rituals of the Goddess
The Tide that Speaks
The Scrolls of Petosiris: 13 Rituals from the Feathered Eye
Petosiris and the Living Plague of Osirion
Feline Fire: Bastet's Passion and Love Magick
The Star Altar of Petosiris
Bastet's Whiskers: Supernatural Sensory Magick
The Bastet Grimoire
Feeding the Shadows
The Mouthless Prayer
The Spiral Wound
Becoming the Ibis: Lessons from Petosiris's Mind
The Crimson Coven: Cola Magick for Sweet Dominion
Sacred Cat's Paw
The Soda Zodiac: A Flavor for Every Sign
Covenant of the Crawling Flame
The Ink of Ish'Zur
Frothroot: The Thirst That Ate the World
The Golden Glyphs of Prosperity
The Etherbind Codex
Echoes of the Resistance: Reclaiming the You That Survived

Harnessed Minds: Breaking Free from Mental Control

The Eyes in the Smoke

Rootwake: The Carbon Covenant

Skitter Logic: Unlearning the Fear That Built You

Doctor Who: The World That Froths

Rootwake: The Fizz That Rewrites Flesh

Rootwake: Frothfather of the World

The Holly Pact: Blood Beneath the Mistletoe

The 2nd Mass Principle: Building Unbreakable Tribes

Web of Wits: A Survival Guide to Encounters with Anasi the Spider (Aunt Nancy)

The Hexbreaking Handbook: Effective Spells to Remove Curses

Pop Alchemy: Transform Your Life One Sip at a Time

The Mason Code: Leading in Unleadable Times

Petosiris and the Fifth Chamber of Thoth

The Ether Seed Within

The Parent of Tomorrow

Petosiris's Pyramid of Perpetual Wealth

Unlearn the World

Grimoire of the Hollow Tongue

Zodiac Weeds: Finding Your Strain Through the Stars

Aquarius Rises in the Bank

The Sugar God's Smile

The Skinclock Reversal: Biohacking the Face of Time

Debtburn: How to Obliterate What You Owe Forever

Get Some Tarot cards: https://www.makeplayingcards.com/sell/ apophis-occult-shop

    <u>Get   some   shirts: https://www.bonfire.com/store/apophis-</u>
<u>shirt-emporium/</u>

<u>**Instagrams:**</u>
@apophis_enterprises,
@apophisbookemporium,
@apophisscardshop
Twitter: @apophisenterpr1
 Tiktok:@apophisenterprise
Youtube: @sg1fan23477
Hive: @sg1fan23477
CheeLee: @SG1fan23477

Podcast: Apophis Chat Zone: https://open.spotify.com/show/5zXbrCLEV2xzCp8ybrfHsk?si=fb4d4fdbdce44dec

Newsletter: https://apophiss-newsletter-27c897.beehiiv.com/

If you want to support me or see posts of other projects that I have come over to: **buymeacoffee.com/mpetchinskg**
I post there daily several times a day

Get your Dinowicca or Christmas themed digital products, especially Santa Raptor songs and other musics. Here:
https://sg1fan23477.gumroad.com

Apophis Yuletide Digital has not only digital Christmas items, but it will have all things with Dinowicca as well as other Digital products.